Good Counsel Press

There Must Be More

F.R.Faller was born in Scotland. A graduate of Glasgow University, he continued his education in English Literature, Communication and Law in Canada and the United States. His background includes the Civil Service, aviation, the oil and energy industries and management consulting.

He has researched and implemented practical ways of assessing self-determination, and improving attitudes to both work and social situations. His central interests lie in clear communication, orderly approaches to decision-making, and personal growth through openness of mind. He provides consulting services to various business sectors and organisations.

F.R.Faller

THERE MUST BE MORE

Good Counsel Press
Inverness

Published in 1988 by
Good Counsel Press
15 Trentham Drive,
Inverness IV1 2TQ
Scotland

Printed and bound in Great Britain by
Bookmag,
A Division of
Highland News Group Ltd
Henderson Road, Inverness

ISBN 0 9513972 0 6

Acknowledgements

There are many contributors to a book of this type, and so many who do not realise where they have contributed. Many of the themes and ideas have developed through several years of professional association with people from all walks of life, all possible situations. Specifically, working environments and the people who played their parts, provided situational focus. Various training, consulting, counselling and group sessions around the world have given otherwise academic material a practical dimension. To the individuals involved, I offer my gratitude.

Special acknowledgements are due to family members and friends who have discussed various issues in self-improvement before and during writing. In particular, I am indebted to the input and encouragement from RSA Symons of Sheffield, and the appreciation of constructive human attitudes from the late Tom Stevenson of Washington State, USA.

CONTENTS

Preface
Introduction

List of Diagrams

PREFACE

This is a self-help manual for people of all backgrounds and circumstances. It is not another success book aimed at executives. Nor is it a formula for becoming a millionaire in two weeks.*There Must Be More* deals with un-pretentious personal growth, working from strengths within the individual. It offers guidance in setting and achieving the right goals, with emphasis on the power of the focused mind.

We often feel that there must be more to life. Tipping the ritual scoop of Corn Flakes into our bowls each morning. Sitting captive in the homebound traffic at the same spot every evening. Finding ourselves irritated with tedious people. Stuck in a job we hate; watching others' success stories; wishing that one day, yes, one day....

The notion of a successful life has many connotations. We could all do better. This has nothing to do with greed or selfishness. Yet goal-setting makes some of us uncomfortable. By limiting ourselves with reservations, we stifle the magnificent potential within us. We also cause others around us to endorse the same restrained outlook. If we freely determine what we truly want, life is not limited, but full of wonder and promise.

Is success a marvellous home or a motor cruiser; a closer relationship with a partner or a parent; control over self-confessed arrogance, or black moods of despair? The prospect of achieving chosen success is exciting. I examined my set of dog-eared life-maps many times. It took courage to admit that my current and desired positions were not the same point. Acting on this realisation was hardest of all. This book helps to redraw your dusty old maps, and select the right bearings. There are no intellectual mountains to be crossed, but prepare yourself for discovery nonetheless.

Oslo, April 1988   FRF

INTRODUCTION

Nothing pleases we humans more than to believe we are living life as we should. If we can at least experience this feeling during good episodes of our lives, we argue that life is not too unfair. This is a reasonable view of things. Unfortunately, it is difficult to maintain this view when we have a prolonged setback, or we begin to seriously question our motives, methods and results.

The quick solution is to subdue our doubts, ambitions and dreams. That is a certain way to disaster, however. We are human; we are dynamic entities. Life is a gift to be used, all the way out to its edges and beyond. The curiosity which led you to buy this book suggests you have come to feel there must be more.

Some fortunate people are sent on seminars by their well-meaning employers. They learn new skills, which directly or indirectly benefit the company. Away from the office environment or the department store, these lucky people learn to delegate work more effectively, or deal with whining customers more graciously. They learn about changing human behaviour. Meanwhile, their harassed managers attend stress reduction workshops, or contemplate Quality Circles translated perfectly from the Japanese. It's all good fun, at least, but hardly self-transforming. Less fortunate individuals seeking to change their lives, consciously choose to attend more growth-specific seminars, paid for by themselves in hard-earned cash.

The more budget-conscious browse around their libraries or bookshops for material which will somehow improve their lives. Newspaper horoscopes are also consulted. It could be that people are natural browsers and dabblers. They find unrelated books on management, selling, IQ testing, or starting their own business. Will the sum of the parts be coherent enough to form a whole? Regardless of the various methods, the truth is: thinking people are constantly on a quest.

Perhaps your boss started it when he asked "Where would you like to be in five years' time?" (Did he know where he would be?). Or maybe you experienced an episode at the traffic lights, when the others saw the green light, but you just sat there. Gear in neutral; mind scheming an escape from daily mediocrity.

There is nothing intrinsically selfish or unsocial about being on a quest. We may, admittedly, undergo doublethink when an agreeable young couple at a party tells us they have just returned from visiting a holy man in India. It is uncommon; we simply cannot relax. There are many quests, but the best are always concerned with human purpose and growth. These two areas have no limits.

This book will not take you further than your desk or the kitchen table. It will not lead you to holy men. It *will* help you to examine yourself more closely than before. Then it will move on to the practical business of deciding what you want in your life, and how you can bring that about. It aims to help you realise, with joy rather than shock or despair, that you are *not* all you could be. I invite you to deal with a serious subject: you.

Life is not a neat set of isolated compartments. People love to think so, but good old change shakes that belief. Rigid ideas which celebrate affluence as the only worthwhile goal of the human race, also face the acid test. If your only aim in life is to get so rich that all other problems can be dealt with (somehow), then be prepared for a tumble at some point. Even the most dedicated high flier must operate among people. Should goals run rough-shod over your best helpers, then you are flying to the crunch. The objective is to arrive with much more than material achievements on display.

The format of the book introduces the material in progressive lessons. Part I (chapters 1 to 4) will help you take stock of your present position, and be more aware of yourself as a person. Part II begins looking ahead to your possible future: chapter 5 provides guidance in determining what you may want from life. Chapter 6 completes the preliminaries by examining fate and other fears facing those wanting to improve their lot. The process of setting realistic life goals, dealing with changes you must make, and the details of *how you will achieve your goals* is explained in Part III (chapters 7, 8 and 9). The last three chapters of Part IV are concerned with review and consolidation of ideas.

You are now setting out on a journey of exploration. Don't worry if you haven't got a complete map. Your next steps will become clear as you move along the road. To make it easier for you, don't take any luggage. (That too will be handled). No need to worry about being spotted by your friends and associates either. You are alone, but in a vast new crowd of friends and associates, all searching just as you are. The journey is not without risk, for you will uncover apathy, laziness, self-doubt and fear. All human growth inflicts a measure of pain, but rarely do trophies fall into our laps by merely waiting.

The person who risks nothing, does nothing, has nothing, is nothing, and becomes nothing. He may avoid suffering and sorrow, but he simply cannot learn and feel and change and grow and love and live. He has forfeited his freedom. Only the person who risks is truly free.

(Anonymous)

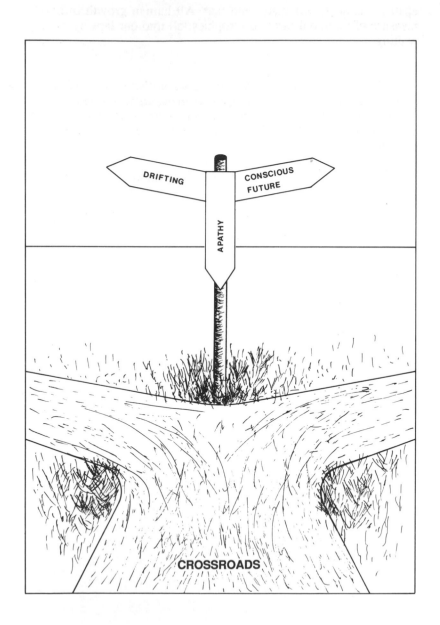

Part I

Where are you right now?

"I've so many things on, I can't think straight".

"Self-help books usually give me a lift if they're any good, but that's as far as I ever get".

"My bed was made long ago; now I must lie in it. Changing things now would be impossible".

"I'm not all that happy, but then it's a comfortable rut I'm in".

"People know me as I am. Isn't that my natural self?"

"Some people like me, some don't. I'm the same with them. It seems to work".

One

The Open Person

If you are wanting to achieve anything with your life, start by being honest with yourself. Accept life gladly, as it happens. Accept the past, but experience today. If the present is unpleasant for you, learn from the experience of it right now. When the time comes, move on to something better. Open up channels within yourself which help you to put all things into healthy perspective. It is difficult to be completely open with others, but why not be open with yourself?

Regardless of what you may believe, you are indeed a free person. The expectations set upon you by others are really not as pervasive as you might think. Your own fundamental truths and philosophies of life are not cast in stone; they are suppositions real to you, for the moment.

We allow our freedom to become compromised with nothing substantial in return. Be yourself and believe in yourself. Who said that your life must go on precisely as it does at present? If you are completely fulfilled and want nothing more, then be happy. If that is not the case, be happy in the fact that there are alternatives for you.

My challenge in writing this book lies in capturing the attention and imagination of your mind. Communication is indeed a clumsy and inadequate instrument. As humans, we are suspicious of any outsider attempting to get inside our minds. We have so many secrets and dark corners in there! Unfortunately, language is the only tool we have, however formal and distant. Ideas may be interpreted wrongly, and any hope of discussion is a non-starter. With these negative aspects at least appreciated, let's try to make a fair attempt at what openness is all about.

If you are going to grow as a person, whether you intend to be a tycoon or a saint, you have to be open to life, and to revising your interpretation of it. What would you say if you were told there was nothing wrong with the world, and nothing right with it either? The statement is senseless? Surrealism is for the birds? Well, I admit there is no simple answer. At least, not for the Open Person.

Before you even begin to grow into an Open Person, your mind needs to know that something is different with you these days. Tell your mind that you require a bit of consideration for a change, that you need more flexibility instead of fixed suppositions. Go on, try it.

Be open and willing to contemplate and try new approaches. For want of a better philosophy, "What is there to lose?" works very well. There is a chance of growth for you, without dark unknowns spoiling your early enthusiasm. Any fears you may have are usually manageable. For example, suspicion of others "using data against you" bothers many people. We fear that by opening up just once, they will tell everyone we're over the edge! We feel that opening up in many situations leads to vulnerability; the other's advantage, our getting hurt. Generally, our fears are out of proportion and damaging to our self-identity.

At the other extreme, making an outright fool of yourself is generally not socially acceptable, especially in certain societies, communities or groups. We are obliged to play the "always in control" game. It might be acceptable (and forgiveable) for ladies at their office stag to grab the male stripper and discover he blushes. But there is always an element of nervousness, self-consciousness and personal insecurity behind the things we will or will not do, and where and when we do them. To overstep boundaries foolishly can invite criticism. In some settings, too much openness is viewed as aggression, disturbing people rather unpleasantly.

Do you find that you conceal this book from your partner, your friends, your boss? Does the subject-matter cause you to be slightly embarrassed, a piece of evidence that you are perhaps less than you should be and you're trying to catch up? Leave a cookbook on the sofa and you'll get no reaction. Leave this book there and welcome your chance to be open! How will you explain yourself? After your feelings of discomfort are out of the way, tell them you want to change yourself by being open to all possibilities. You might discover that the Open Person must be open enough to suffer incredulous friends who stereotype you as someone who really does need help!

To be open is to be human. To be human, we do share sensitive self-knowledge at times, at least with family or trusted friends. We need to overcome fear of rejection, fear of criticism, fear of losing self-balance. Strong identifications with peer groups or role models may have to be dismantled, or they will keep us as we are.

We can appreciate our own inadequacies while celebrating our real potential. You will discover again what it really means to be honest. Honesty is a human problem, an uncomfortable hang-up. When do we know we are honest with ourselves? How do we *really* know how we feel? Are our opinions or world view honest enough to rely on?

You might notice it easier to be honest with other people than with yourself (because you sense if you are lying to others). This is an area to contemplate and work at. For our present purposes, try not to lie to others, and do try to be honest with yourself!

Be open with yourself. Make a quick list of the personal faults you know cause you problems. Here's a list of prompts to get you started:

Serious outlook on life causes me to moan and whine

Frustration with tedious people or situations

Sarcastic and sharp with people

Self-centred more than selfish

Standoffish, trace of snobbery and disapproval

Very suspicious of strangers, any environment

Difficulty in letting go, relaxing

Sense of humour clouded by grey outlook

Trace of sourness over life's problems and setbacks

If you were an Open Person, you would feel able to put your list on the wall at work, give your partner one, pin one to the squash club notice board, and place it as a personal advertisement in your local rag. Try some sensitive hang-ups you probably have on material wealth and ambition. Again, some quick prompts:

I'll never clear my mortgage this side of the grave

Lady Luck never calls on me

Owning a new car isn't a reality

My family were always losers

Two years of unemployment has fixed me for good

I have no contacts, no education, no money

Why do some people get the boats and fancy cars?

It's wrong to always want more than you have

I just seem to suit a rut, well, it's predictable

These are typical admissions that we would rather keep close counsel on. We might declare ourselves ambitious and confident high fliers to the world. Inside, we might be snivelling, self-persecuting defeatists waiting to be hit by the proverbial bus. To make any progress in the ways you had intended, come clean about the very things that cause you a bit of pain. Write them down and see them looking up at you (that tends to dull their power over you). So many people soldier on, carrying albatrosses about with them. "I'm a failure, so don't keep nagging at me! I can prove to you I can't do any better!"

We tend to have fixed attitudes and approaches to things. We find lazy ways of dealing with our everyday challenges, whether they are demanding or trivial. A car stalls ahead of us. Do we move around it, sit there blasting the horn, or accept the situation and wait till the car starts? Or is there even the possibility of getting out and helping? The least troublesome course usually wins for the vast majority of people. We have a sad lack of basic comprehension and initiative when it comes to external situations. We have few spontaneous mechanisms to handle them. Becoming involved is seldom an option; we justify our inaction rather than acting. The projection of this everyday behaviour into our own lives causes personal growth suffocation.

t	l	a	c	w	a	t	d	a
a	e	r	h	h	r	o	o	n
u	s	e	a	i	e		e	
g	s	n	c	h		a	s	o
h		n	g	h	o	c	n	p
t	o	o	e		r	c	’	e
	p	t		a	g	e	t	n
t	e		a	r	a	p		
o	n	m	t	e	n	t	c	m
	-	e		i			o	i
r	m	a	w	d	s	t	m	n
e	i	s	i	i	e	h	e	d
a	n	u	l	f	d	a		.
d	d	r	l	f		t	e	a
	e	a	.	i	i		a	h
l	d	b	t	c	n	o	s	,
i	;	l	h	u		u	y	w
k	t	y	e	l	p	r	.	e
e	h		t	t	a		y	l
	e	m	c		t	m	o	l
t	y	o	h	t	t	i	u	,
h		r	i	o	e	n		t
i	w	e	n		r	d	h	h
s	e		e		n	s	a	a
.	r	o	s		s		v	t
	e	r	e				e	

Can you interpret anything from this matrix of letters? As you tackle the problem, consider the logical steps you took before deciding how it finally worked. Did you feel a sense of frustration, even for a moment?

Certain accepted stimuli can be effective in helping us to become more open. For example, music allows us to relax some inhibitions. We can join in to some extent, humming, whistling, moving our hands to an imaginary orchestra, or playing a make-believe guitar at a fantasy rock concert. The Arts help us, as far as we want to go. Theatre commands our sense of abandon with artistic licence; it is socially acceptable to explain why *Waiting For Godot* holds special insights for us. Similarly, nature and love of the outdoors is considered safe as a conversation piece, providing you don't get too militant about saving whales, or screaming incessantly about acid rain.

These stimuli and topics are quite tame: they allow us to sample and discuss life without coping with it. The Arts, for example, keeps the action of the stage or the painter's creativity at a safe distance. We readily tolerate unusual people, ambiguities and absurd possibilities in a play or a painting. Psychedelic departures, or even a little dabbling with madness, is acceptable in a detached setting.

To remain open to such things in our everyday lives is quite different! We deal with our own ambiguities or hang-ups by keeping them to ourselves, or "in the family". Meeting the same things in others, is decidedly uncomfortable.

We may take great pride in declaring ourselves to be open-minded; this is wrongly analogous to saying we are modern in outlook. So many old established customs and social attitudes have altered in our own lifetime. Consider the changes in divorce law, religious convictions, treatment of the mentally ill, and sexual freedom. It is inevitable that these and other human attitudes will keep changing; the pendulum of popular morality will no doubt swing too.

The older generation feels comfortable with the values and patterns they chose to live by. As new ways appear, they find them strange, threatening, and destructive in many instances. The development of collective and individual consciousness in the sixties was viewed by some as a breakthrough; by others, a downward slide of western civilisation. The seventies was a period of retraction, a consolidation of the *me* mentality. This return to a nominally stable, conservative world view, a move to accepting responsibility rather than rejecting it, was seen by many as a return to sanity. Hence the emergence of the politics of "tried-and-tested common sense" on both sides of the Atlantic.

Attitudes in the eighties are different again. Perhaps we cannot pass judgement on them until the nineties are well under way. It is clear, however, that our personal consciousness grows up around concurrent states of safety and fear, whatever generation, political ideology or world view we like to associate with. The present generation feeds off old ideas (outward morality to mask irresponsibility), recent ideas (qualifying instead of dropping out), and current ideas (perhaps apathy of the eighties?).

Whenever we associate with a given pattern, a set of values, or a consciousness we feel safe with, there are two significant poles to consider. First, the comforting reality of feeling at home with patterns that give life some form. We can "think straight" and behave ourselves predictably. Second: the problems of shifting to an opposing or "new, untried, ambiguous, threatening" pattern. Both poles are in tension, of course.

It might be a moral, political or scientific issue. If we are firm believers in Position A, how can we feel comfortable with Position B? This is where the dichotomy is born. A watershed of essential but awkward division in our very process of thinking.

So how can there possibly be such a reality as "Open Thinking" or "Open People"? We are all tied in knots by our own special selection of patterns and attitudes. Did you have trouble with the Chinese pattern of reading? To be an Open Person, be willing *to set aside* your trusted patterns of thought and behaviour. That does not mean you are going to become a dissident of some sort, nor that you will float about agreeing with everyone and everything. The Open Person is one who makes a conscious decision to embrace the other person's view, without necessarily agreeing with it. Bigots just won't succeed in this exercise, nor will fanatics of any calling. Flat-earth enthusiasts should do very well (if they can accept the world *might* be spherical for a day now and then).

As you move through an average day, people and situations will present themselves to you. Whether you think they are significant or not, become aware of your own thoughts, every hour, every moment. Try this for a whole day, attempting to keep "open" to every single piece of experience which comes your way. How many times did you have difficulties with the basic thought-patterns arising from other people or situations? Did you have to remind yourself you were being "open" that day, as we agreed? Not all days turn up manifestations in Truth, but if you're open enough, you might be surprised.

There was a new notice on the bulletin board. It was quite long, professionally done on yellow paper, with striking artwork and typeset letters. I glanced at the heading:

ROCK AROUND THE WORLD

I had talked to Adrian twice before about his use of the firm's graphic supplies for "government" jobs. This time he had gone too far. The notice was worth more than some work for clients. It was clear he was just trying this one on. Making his point against my recent promotion to supervisor. He was a popular fellow, reasonably good at his job, but becoming a real Prima Donna.

On the way to the art department, I met our receptionist, Anne. We nodded as we passed; then I stopped.

"Oh, Anne, could I have a word?"

"Certainly".

"Have you seen Adrian's notice?"

"Ah, yes, it's good isn't it? I think he hit the spot with the girls. The guys are too stuffy, don't you think?"

I knew that meant me too; over the hill and all that. Without much more than a Hhrrmph! I proceeded to arty little Adrian's world of paints and sticky papers. He was leaning over his table.

"This notice on the board, what's wrong with your memory? Or are you half deaf? You arty types, you're all the same! I remember art students at college: they were hippies alright! All show and no responsibility! Well, I'm afraid this...."

Adrian calmly reached to a pile of loose papers. He handed me one sheet, yellow. I glanced down and began to read.

ROCKIN' ALL OVER THE WORLD

Your favourite band (and mine) are still alive
and appearing at Wembley

!!! STATUS QUO !!!
In the company of
BOB GELDOF AND FRIENDS
At the occasion of
RELIEVING SUFFERING
Among wonderful people on this very earth
That were forgotten as a result of
OUR CLOSED MINDS
But we have remembered
OUR COMPASSION, OUR LOVE AND OUR CASH

Contact Adrian
Art Department

Work pressures are particularly effective at keeping us from being open. Imagine engineers, scientists or undertakers being open in their professions! Managers and supervisors in any work environment feel they must keep that essential distancing phenomenon alive and active. Become too familiar and divulge your little idiosyncrasies to your peril! You may be faced with accusations of weakness, a hierarchal plot against you, or daily snubs from the very staff you confided in. They do love you, but very conditionally.

Is it really like this? The Open Person must learn how to live in this real world, but remain true to inner convictions. The secret is to deal honestly with the dichotomy, between what *is* and what you are *becoming*. People may not give a hoot about your developing inner mind or your secret desire to become a world-class jockey! But don't allow their indifference to limit you in any way.

When you go about your affairs, try to keep an open mind on developments which are completely unplanned and out of the blue. You might miss something vitally important if you shut your mind to unexpected events.

-If a friend asks you to go out in his or her sailing dinghy, go. You might hate getting frozen and wet, but something else will make the day a success.

-Don't routinely criticise your daughter's taste in music. Play a few albums and take it all in. See what is real there, for her. It might help you to communicate with her weird friends (are they *so* weird?).

-If you fancy an outfit in a January sale, but it's just *not* the type of thing people normally see you wearing, buy it!

-When you meet two women at a party discussing Tarot cards and astrology, ask them what they think, even if you feel that it's all nonsense.

-If you go to a library, force yourself to take books from shelves you've never explored before.

-If you have a thing about women in the workplace who drive the fork-lifts, talk with them.

-If you don't like the idea of male nurses, have a pint with a dozen of them!

Men with ear-rings get to you? Black lipstick? Loud clothes? Do you feel inadequate around senior executives? Are you having problems accepting different races, religions, or sexual preferences? Do children leave you cold and you can't understand them? Are you ignoring certain people for some peculiar reason you hold dear? No need to walk in their shoes, but *listen to them* for a change.

Are you snagged in a daily routine? Change it! Take the bus sometimes instead of the car. Take a taxi just for a treat. Try walking. Do you eat meat-and-two-veg because that's what your mother fed you forty years ago? Eat chili or tacos or lasagne! Are you fed up doing the work you've done for twenty years? Then open up your mind to what else you might be able to do. You make your own rules; why should it be otherwise?

Whenever people went wild about a film, a play, or a show, I consciously downgraded and avoided it. Popular entertainment is so much hype. I felt that *Cats* was a prime example. When I lived in London, the pressure was on to see Cats. I bought tickets, reluctantly. Sitting near the stage, it was impossible to avoid Cats. They were everywhere. Smiling, purring, singing Cats! Despite my early prejudice, I was overcome by the action, lighting, incessant energy, the emotion and magic. It was tremendous!

I decided it was not just another musical; it was a spiritual experience. Sometimes we are given so much, are lifted so high, by the least obvious surprises. It takes so little effort to open up positively to things we have pre-judged. Yet we resist, alas. Andrew Lloyd Webber, keep doing what you do best.

The Open Person recognises and tolerates personal short-comings. The Open Person sees opportunities in all things. Fixed ideas, fixed routines, fixed judgements on everything: they limit you and narrowly define the possibilities of your life. Why do you allow such control over *you?* Are you terrified of living your life to its ultimate potential? If you are going to be on the train, then take your blinkers off and look at the scenery.

A friend insisted I should go with her to the wrestling. The very idea insulted my intelligence! It's all a put-up, the bouts are all rigged, it's ridiculous anyway: you know the sort of thing. I knew she would get sick of it after a few Saturday nights. So on this basis, I went.

It was another world. Like gladiators, some of them. They took it all so seriously, especially the spectators! Women were the ones to watch: they went berserk if their darling boy was getting cabbage ears from a bully. The action eclipsed the futility of each bout. Wiry little hamsters and impossibly fat hippos, waltzing about, trying to pull each other's limbs off. It was insane but delightful. Six Saturday nights at the wrestling reminded me we're quite hopelessly daft, but harmless.

There is nothing in the idea of being open to suggest you must fall in with the people or the things you open up to. If you have some hang-ups on specific issues, you may have to accommodate or suppress them. The important step is to realise what is going on with you: "I have hang-ups on this and that, but I want to understand why it is so".

For example, you may have a "moral" reason for not going to the races at Aintree. Gambling! *That* side of life! Bookies' shops in the High Street! People getting excited over horses, while others can't afford to go out at all! You might be *internally* correct in your judgements, but is that the final reality?

Try going to the races, just once. Bet on a few nags. Take part in the proceedings as if you were playing truant from school. Study the form, and study the people. Witness what happens to them when they see their silly old horse dragging behind the rest. Watch them win. Watch the people studying the parade at the paddock. Eat a greasy hamburger with greasy onions. And watch yourself every moment.

Experience all there is. When the day is done, ask yourself what you really feel about your previous views on racing and racing people. Be assured, God or your conscience will not zap you for betraying your allegiance to morality. *He* will be standing behind you in the queue, studying form, and watching to see which horse *you* think has class.

By giving yourself permission to depart from your usual judgemental routines and ways of thinking, you will begin to see your world a little differently. No sweeping enlightenment, unfortunately. Just a realisation that you are missing huge chunks of yourself, by cutting off areas you decided were off-limits to your experience.

The North American thing is to go on a 3 week trip to take in the Old Country. They fly to Heathrow, then take the tube, because they've heard stories about London cabbies. Their itinerary takes them from Harrod's, to Hastings, the Cotswolds, Stratford-upon-Avon, the Lake District, Edinburgh, the Yorkshire of James Herriot, and back to Heathrow.

I remember asking friends how it went.

"It was Okay. The trains were good, a bit dirty, y'know. Couldn't get a thing to eat. Always closed. Hey, Sunday a guy could starve over there! I think the punks were kinda weird. Everything looked run down. I guess there was a strike on someplace. We just couldn't get warm and their shops don't have air conditioning! Yeah, it was a good trip. We'll do Italy or Greece next year maybe".

I think all travellers fall into three classes: business, tourist and adventurer. Business people fail to notice where they are. It could be the Raffles Hotel in Singapore, the Hilton in Bombay, or the Tropicana in Santa Barbara. Hotels and taxis have become identical worldwide. Tourists are bored where they are *now*, and they have surplus money to throw at something. So a break away from the daily routine is as good as anything. Hence the sardine syndrome on Spanish beaches.

Adventurers set out on a quest, prepared for surprises. They might end up running a boatyard in Thailand, or counting reindeer near Skoganvarre. Adventurers have no reservations; they just stay open and miss nothing. *Everyone* is a potential adventurer.

What if you were told that 80% of you could be unrealised, uncharted, missing? Send out the search party! Certainly, each person has their own realistic level of awareness, and capacity to be open. By opening more, we always increase our awareness and potential. So begin your quest by being open. Shut out possibilities with your mind, and you end up with a small, limited mind. Open up beyond the obvious, and you will see there's much more to you than you have allowed. You will not be seeking your potential outside yourself. What you need is *already within you.* Grasping that will be your greatest step forward.

Two   Are You Aware of Yourself?

Whatever lifestyle you lead, you would probably admit that our lives are generally busy. Even if you are spending your time in prison, there is a daily routine to occupy your time. On TV, we often watch busy executives jetting around making fantastic deals, then rushing home to their busy families. In less glamorous settings, there are many overloaded mothers, coping with children to and from school. Shopping, part-time job, entertaining friends, trying to stay trim with Jane Fonda tapes blasting away.

How often do you get a real break from a *busy mind?* Trying to sleep with a busy mind is one situation we are all familiar with. Problems, bad recollections of the day's events, reminiscences or past relationships. All fluttering about like crazed birds the cat brought into the house. Sometimes there's a silly tune you can't drop from your consciousness. You look at the clock. Three a.m. Maybe a visit to the bathroom. You'll be drained tomorrow. The symptoms of a busy mind; refusing to settle.

Of course, the busier we are, in general terms, the less time we have to think about life and its undisclosed possibilities. Why spend time contemplating your navel when there's films to see, people to visit, cars to drive, boats to sail, paths to jog, and worries to entertain? Being perpetually busy keeps our minds off things, and that can't be bad. (Or so we hope). Whenever the basic questions of "who and what are you?" arise, you answer by saying "it's time I did the ironing, it's overdue".

The quiet moments cause the most trouble! If you are very unfortunate, you may experience short flashes of "presence". In other words, you suddenly become aware of where you are and what you are experiencing. You are standing on the bus with your wrist through a strap, thinking "*this is me on the bus,* and I feel conspicuous".

Accidents are good at bringing us into the immediacy of the present. Crises in our lives put us outside ourselves, as if we were a spectator at our own tragedies. Even if you cut a finger while peeling onions, there is an awareness of your own body; blood leaks from it, and your concern focuses on the moment. It vanishes of course, as you race to find the sticking plaster and human comfort. There are other, less violent ways to discover we are really here, fortunately. And that assumes we look in the right places.

Our presence on this earth is quite often defined or substantiated by other people. The people around you have decided who you are and what makes you tick, at least to the limits of their interest in you. They have even specified rules of behaviour which you have grown into. How helpful people really are!

Are you aware of what the essential you is? Is it mostly your job, your cynicism with everything about you, your easy-going banter, the feeling of being a good parent, your prowess in athletics or sexual encounters? Is it the way people look to you for advice, the stories you tell, your stability, your chaos, your brilliant mind or your bank balance?

You are known for those things. You perpetuate their opinions of *you* through the consistent practice of the things you do. You communicate signals that other people pick up, rightly or wrongly. Signals can be misleading. They often relate only to specific people and environments. For example, eating out, you may be perceived as a fusspot; at home, a slob. Travelling on planes, you are an aggressive pig; on trains, a real saint. Your workmates see you as reliable, true to the firm and a great person to be with; at home, you might be a broody, self-centred troublemaker that people in their right mind should avoid. Socially, you might be a friend to all in pubs, but the poisoned one that causes social clubs and cricket teams to disband. When we try to understand how other people see us, we catch various glimpses of what they think we are really like. It is indeed a series of conflicting images in a wobbly mirror. Quite often, we believe in the wrong reflected image.

The real danger lies in other people defining what we are and *limiting* us as a result. It can develop to extremes. For example, I remember an employer who was dumbfounded on hearing that a certain man was an accomplished public speaker in local politics. The poor chap was kept out of sight in stores because they thought he was a mouse.

It would be nice to *tell* people that we are not mice; and for them to give us a fair chance to be ourselves. The main problem of course, is that we have really not decided what we want to be known *as*. Our image has been built since childhood, and for the most part, we allowed it to happen, seeing no reason for change. Rather than question how our image was developing, it was easier and less troublesome to have others reflect possibilities that were near enough to make no difference. This is acceptable when we are younger, but can become an identity crisis in later life. You are presently exploring the reality of change, and how the future is going to see you, are you not?

Sudden changes in attitude or behaviour will naturally strain your relationships with others, and will certainly raise a few eyebrows. You might be a quiet, reserved soul that lives like a recluse. If you suddenly appear out there tomorrow as a gregarious, insufferable socialite, you are going to see some interesting adjustments! It seldom happens this way, fortunately. Your self-growth will be more ordered and allows for transition.

The pressures to satisfy another's image of you are tremendous. Doing something as an individual now and then brings you back to the reality of you actually *being* here. Other people like to see you *just so*. It makes life simpler for them. Once they have established and fixed who you are, they can deal with you over and over again, without having to start from scratch. It is a social convention, but it stifles your vitality. People do it to us, and the worst thing of all, *we do it to ourselves*.

I think my marriage has gone stale. Maybe it's me. I'm well aware that I married too young, and looking back, I should have studied or something. Why didn't I train as a nurse or a legal secretary? I liked art. Perhaps I could have become a dress designer, or a commercial artist with an advertising agency. How about editor of a woman's magazine?

I'll be 36 next month. I certainly don't *feel* old. I don't think I like myself as I used to. My husband is a good provider; I doubt if he even considers other women. He sees me as someone who organises the house; I'm just a social necessity. All *he* needs to do is work away, and give me money for the hairdresser's or winter boots.

The kids drain me now; they're challenging me all the time. I'm bored with women who talk houses and dishwashers and soap powders. I'm trapped, doing the same old things, getting no satisfaction or fun out of life.

If I could only get a full-time job at something I'd like. I have talent! I'm intelligent! Part-time in a newsagent's is the end. I'll need an income if I'm going to go it alone. Something's got to happen; this can't go on forever.

People I talk to make it clear they don't want to hear my problems. You see it in their faces. Another drudge pining about the lost years, dreaming of being an airline captain or a marketing executive. I wish I had a really close friend to give me some clues. There's *got* to be more than this. I must be good at something. I wish I could find the energy to concentrate on finding a way. Honestly, I'm tired.

This distressed lady is convinced the marriage is at the centre of her problems. She laments her lost opportunities. She blames her husband. She blames her friends for being so shallow. She blames the system for stacking the odds against women like her. Though she believes the time has come to be independent, she has no commercially recognisable skills or earning capacity. She feels she has talent, but that is subjective. There are no clear ideas on how to achieve any of her possible plans. Her age is certainly on her side. She could learn the skills she needs to fulfil herself in a career/interest sense. She could *choose* to avoid women that make soap powders their level of fascination, and find new friends.

What has actually happened here is less obvious and will take much more effort to solve. The husband has reached an understanding of his wife over many years, which basically suits him. He's the provider; he probably likes his work. Other women aren't his scene. He has the basics in place (lovely wife, kids, house, job, good standard of living, *lifestyle*). He feels satisfied that she talks to other women about harmless things. He believes her outlet at the newsagent's lets her meet people and circulate a bit.

She has lost herself somewhere along the way. As a girl, she met this man, fell in love, and married him. Then the kids, the house, the lifestyle based largely on his job. His identity is probably well established and visible at work. Home is largely her domain. Her identity was sacrificed willingly, but unwittingly. Whatever interest she had in art was lost too. Has she explained her feelings of stagnation as a person to her husband? Is he aware of the sacrifice she has made for their cosy but boring lifestyle? Her needs as an individual person have been frustrated, but like most things in life, individuals are responsible for making choices and taking action.

Both partners assumed they were doing the right things for so long. They had created each other's roles and they acted them, as they were expected to. Following the script was the easy option. The status quo was being maintained. Undoing all this, or questioning motives, would have caused pain.

Marriages are not protected in any special way from stereotyping roles. We may learn to tolerate stereotypes in the workplace, but not in a marriage. Social conventions often stifle the vitality of individuals in a relationship. Even more tragic, the partnership itself may die. It is time this couple stood outside the images they have allowed to grow on themselves. It will certainly mean all cards being placed on the table, then dealing with painful realities and coping with the stresses of change. Marriages are miniature societies, with great scope for all to grow, providing the effort is made. How often we avoid pain, only to suffer worse consequences!

Can *you* shake off the imaginary you that's ingrained so deeply? Is there such a thing as a fresh start? Of course there is! The first step is to determine who you are inside, then promise yourself to be flexible about the next steps. Your age or circumstances *are immaterial*. A vital part of the exercise is establishing the awareness of *presence:* I really am here. The situation of trying to be someone else, or squeezing yourself into some mould, is unhealthy. We need to be acknowledged as the people we are, to enjoy being alive, and to achieve something with what we have. Whenever you are misrepresented, compromised or ignored, say so.

When you are about your everyday life, are you aware of the realities of the moment? Have you concrete feelings of *being?* Yes I know it's abstract, but think about it. For example: I am reading this book, I am talking, I am peeling potatoes, I am flying an aircraft, I am being an utter fool, I am kissing my lover, I am in a lift with strangers, I am crying, I am laughing, I am feeling depressed....you might call it the "this is it" reality. Good, bad, happy, sad. Whatever is happening to you at the moment; now, any time. Experience it completely. Savour it like the smell of good baking or the headiness after passing your driving test.

Imagine yourself attending an interview, but not for a job. Let's say it's some research on the nature of people these days. After an hour of discussing yourself (in any way you think appropriate), what would the panel's notes look like? Write up some quick notes from their side of the table. Did you see yourself sitting there? Did you hear the awkward things you decided to tell them? What sort of person were you: how aware, how straightforward?

If you rush about all day, forever occupied and "involved", you will miss the whole point of being in touch with the moment. Too much rushing and you'll lose yourself in the draught. How much of your time is really wasted, should you look at it objectively? If not exactly wasted, are there periods of time which give you very little in terms of being that specially unique person, *you?*

Making money and spending it might make you happy in a general sense, but is the process a joy to you? Think about your feelings whenever you do anything. You will find you even have feelings cutting grass with a lawn-mower, or watching a sparrow playing in a hedge. These things, trivial as they are, should not be dismissed as trivia unworthy of a place in your consciousness. Feelings are *your* feelings. You feel them, and you are alive because of them. It isn't possible to learn how to feel, in the same way we learn how to perform a job of work. But it is possible to acknowledge what is happening inside you, as a result of experiences around you.

When in a crowd, do you feel lost in it? Do you feel self-conscious, detached from it in some way, or even feel superior to it? When people are surrounded by people, they can feel lonelier or more conspicuous than on a mountain-top. If you were called on to make a speech at a presentation or a community gathering, would you feel their eyes on you? The awareness of self is often intensified by situations such as these. Don't fight it! You exist!

Life can be seen as absurd nonsense, or a thrill. You may drift along if you want, but drift along properly. When things happen around you, take it all in. Don't limit your encounters only to good things; we can learn so much from troubles also, even if the experience runs us ragged. Examine your feelings and acknowledge they are there. If a film makes you sentimental, and you allow that feeling to flood your consciousness, let it enrich you. Don't question your motives or deny yourself the chance of learning through direct experience. Limit emotion and you limit experience, creativity, life. Through feelings, you give yourself clear evidence that *you are here and there's stuff in you,* rather than rushing around merely coping with life. Laugh at yourself, whatever your predicament. Study situations when they go wrong, and patiently monitor events for things you might normally miss.

Be assertive when you must be assertive; don't let people walk all over you. But never slip into aggression: that is unproductive and unhealthy. Explain things to those who need to be informed of how you feel, what you think. It is so much easier in the long run *growing as we go.* Major overhauls are stressful and usually costly in terms of fall-out. Don't deny your feelings or your presence in any situation (but allow others the same). Politely refuse to fit into the rigid patterns of others, just to keep the peace or make life easy. Why live your life if you cannot honestly say it is yours?

Being you is easy, and yet it's the most difficult thing! You can go on as you have been doing, or you can reach for the stars. You are at the centre of all you are; have you noticed? You will have setbacks and problems trying to get this right. But the effort in trying will be rewarded. Your desire to be fully in touch with yourself must come before hopes, goals and ambitions. Otherwise, you are off to a false start. You are not empty-handed. The power to attain is *within* you. The time to begin is today, in preparation for tomorrow.

Three   Preparing an Inventory: Things

The idea of this chapter is to define your material worth in some detail. It will help you to assess your attitudes to the possessions you have, and those you may want to have. There is no scoring system as such: you are simply taking a good look at the material aspect of your life. Include everything that has tangible value (but don't labour over the possible value of your vast butterfly collection). While playing the accountant, take time to reflect on what it all means to you. Do you think you want lots more, or would you happily give some away?

We all gather things in our time here. As we progress through our several phases, we gather possessions. In childhood there are toys, games and novelties. In adolescence there is a tendency to relate possessions to learning, hence the proliferation of home computers, musical instruments and reading materials. Then the electronic novelties, including hi-fi's and cassette players. When we graduate to the more serious consumer years, the list is infinite. Advertising and social pressures feed the urge to consume, to participate.

There was a time when the United States was recognised as the model society for collecting, using, and enjoying possessions. It was easy to wag the finger of indifference at their materialistic way of life. Many Americans, and Europeans, in their growing awareness of the past decades, have come to question the blind demand for material goods. They agree that materialism in itself does not necessarily improve the quality of life. Yet it is so very difficult in our structured societies to release our attachment to possessions.

Regardless of the amount of information we have on the in-equalities of our world, we must attend to our own affairs. In our everyday situations, we cannot be held responsible for earthquakes, famines or disasters. But then we are welcome, as humans, to *respond* to such things in the world. Whether you are rich or poor is immaterial. If you want to help, please help. There is a surfeit of unfounded and unproductive guilt all around us. It is a human thing to sometimes feel uneasy about our relative prosperity and privilege. This is something we all must cope with. If you are to make any sense of your material position, you must feel comfortable and grateful in the reality of owning things. *Then* consider what you are going to do about the world. Wallowing in the injustices of the world makes us miserable and does nothing to improve our individual or collective lot.

How many of us in the Western world could live as pleasantly after our hot water systems, refrigerators, washing machines, home heating appliances, televisions, radios, hi-fi's, coffee percolators, electric lawn-mowers, cars, sewing machines and electric razors were taken from us? Electric toothbrushes, powered carving knives or food processors might be more easily sacrificed before releasing the necessities!

By the same token, if you have a humble but friendly little flat of your own, or a very nice place indeed thankyou on the Thames, would you gladly share a twelve-foot caravan on the Northumberland moors? Now there is nothing wrong with living in a caravan. If you are happy, it is ideal. However, if you are in a caravan, but would like a nice bungalow, don't feel guilty about it! That is the spirit in which we should embrace material things. Like them, but never exactly love them.

Returning to your list. Only you know what you have. What you must do is gather your thoughts and behave like an accountant. To give you some assistance in this exercise, refer to the *Inventory: Things* tables. Follow the outlines given and tabulate or estimate the value of each and every thing you list. Should your items not fit the list as shown, improvise, but don't miss anything important. If you have a yacht moored off Monaco, don't forget to list that too. If it's a one-fifth share in a greyhound with premature atherosclerosis, put it down (but be kind to the dog). We are doing an audit of your net worth, whether you're in a mansion or a bedsit.

Net worth must consider the debts as well as the assets. (Now the truth comes out). In the section on outstanding loans, list mortgages or other charges against your assets. There is no point hoping the loan from your brother will somehow go away, just because he earns more than you. *Don't live under illusions. Know the worst, face up to it, and plan accordingly.* (As an Open Person, you should have no difficulty being forthright).

If you have been honest with yourself, you will have a very good idea of where you currently stand. Deduct your total liabilities from assets (assume all loans called by the banks, building societies and brothers). You now have your net worth for our purposes here. That is the first milestone in your material inventory. You have established some worthwhile facts about yourself.

Tangible things are not simply possessions that can be turned into hard cash. There are other important aspects of your net worth that must be considered. The potential to make money and translate effort into possessions is a hidden asset most people ignore.

Are you employed? Would you call it a career or a job? Gainful work is a substantial component in our self-perception and position in life. If you are unemployed, you are still required to take part in the assessment. Unemployment is merely a state of not having a job or doing gainful work. It is not the thing itself that is so bad, but the artificially imposed sense of separation that goes with it. So, working or not, what does work mean to you? Is it simply a case of regular money coming in, or status? Does it satisfy you completely, or are you generally at odds with work? In general terms, what value do you place on work? Give it more than a quick thought. Try to focus on the potential of work as a real asset, not just the present value.

Just as assets less liabilities told you something, your monthly income less outgoings results in net monthly excess. Think about your monthly income from all sources (salary, unemployment benefit, family allowance, bank interest, share dividends, moonlighting). Then consider where most of it goes (mortgage, rent, food, heating, car expenses, insurance, clothing, entertainment, petfood, loan payments). The amount left after the deductions is your net monthly excess. See table *Monthly Income and Expenses*. Is it positive or negative?

Depending on *how* positive or negative this number is, it is obvious that your personal lifestyle is closely governed and measured by the economics of money in, money out. If you live frugally on a low income, you might be as well off as the big spenders on big salaries. The real difference is only one of scale, and probably the degree of personal anxiety.

What is *your* personal lifestyle? That is as diverse a question as there are people. If your net worth and your net monthly excess are both looking very sorry, don't despair! This exercise was planned to bring you to a true and impartial understanding of your material situation. I have no hidden agenda to place you above or below some arbitrary benchmark.

The process also determines your realistic lifestyle based on current assets and earning power. If you are a company director in the top 500 group of companies, you can still feel miserable after this exercise. Quite often, top people are the very ones to take unreasonably big risks to hit the big time. Their visible numbers on paper may be significant, but so might be their worry with the debt-load to keep up appearances. Living beyond your means is not true success. Any plausible citizen can collect loans and credit leverage. There is no competitive allusion here. It is a process of self-discovery and personal assessment at the most basic level: things. Notice that no comment is being made on what you *should* have, or what ratios *must* be in place between capital assets and your expenditures. We are only establishing a point on your map.

How do you *feel* about your Net Worth? Are you content, feeling really smug at how well-off you are? Do you feel vulnerable, subject to the least ill wind that could destroy you financially and every other way? If you lost your present monthly income, how long would it take before things would have to change significantly? Are your reserves in terms of years, months or weeks? How independent of the system do you perceive yourself to be? Are you mortgaged so deeply that you could lose your home should you be made redundant? If you are struggling along in the middle of a crisis at the moment, are you holding your own or steadily going down every week? Are you so self-sufficient that you are quite bored with money altogether, and would gladly become a weaver in Skye, just to escape the nonsense of it all? To help you in gauging your feelings to all this, you must tell yourself the whole story on paper. Writing the situation down concentrates your feelings beautifully.

You alone know where you stand right now. Be honest. Be angry if you wish. Be singularly complacent if you believe that this whole exercise has been tedious and beneath you. You are free to be whatever is appropriate. Some of you might have discovered how emotional you became as a result of calculating your position, and taking time to think about it. Remember, the numbers themselves are only relative. It's how you feel about them that really adds up. Furthermore, understand that you can do something to change your position, if you so decide. In setting goals later, you will re-visit your feelings from this exercise.

Ask yourself if all those possessions and sources of income are important to you, or do they only add up to responsibility, worry, and fear of loss. Buddha said:*The less you have, the less you have to worry about.* You don't have to be a Buddhist to see the truth in that. There is so much clutter in our lives. Separating the *things you really want* from clutter is an exacting task. This book will not lead you to a lifestyle or possessions that are not meant for you. What would be the point of that?

Examine your net worth and net monthly excess relative to the lifestyle you lead, and to the *lifestyle you might want to lead.* Try not to equate lifestyle with mere luxury and excitement. (Some very rich and successful people have very mundane hobbies. Conversely, some very unremarkable people have a love of exquisite things, whether they can own them or not). It is a fallacy that the bottom line is *always* money.

There is a spiteful trap awaiting us, when our logic leads us to blindly assume that someone else's lifestyle is better than ours. "Oh, but they've got more money than us, they're on the up and up". We inflict unhappiness on ourselves when we superimpose inappropriate values which embarrass our finite resources. There is a constant internal battle between our desires and our frustration at not getting them. Concentrate on yourself before you compare notes with what everyone else has, or does. You may fancy that fellow's Ferrari, but why? *Why?* Just because it's an unmistakable symbol?

There is also a dangerous and unproductive force in that peculiar trait of humankind: equating money, behaviour or things with status. A man wears a visibly expensive tailored suit, a Crombie overcoat and a silk scarf. He is seen stepping into a smart white Mercedes, illegally parked outside a smart Knightsbridge shop. Why must we confer on him more status than Mr. Average? Not content with that, passers-by feel they have more status than the van driver trying to park his vehicle behind the Mercedes. All the while, the van driver is feeling particularly superior that day, relative to traffic wardens. Why must "money mentality" influence the passage of events, as experienced by the four "tiers" of people? It's ludicrous!

Net worth is a phenomenon of our vanity in many cases. It specifies at a point in time where we are financially, in terms of possessions, and arguably, lifestyle. Nevertheless, keep your mind open to the whole picture. This book is not about to make you rich using some secret formula or sham hocus-pocus, nor prescribe money as the cure-all for human misery and restlessness. If you have thought carefully about the searching interrogatories here, you will have recognised which path you are probably on. Right now, you know what things you have, and what those things mean to you. Later, we can examine what you would like to have. Isn't that a happy prospect?

INVENTORY: THINGS (ASSETS)

ASSETS   *AMOUNT OR ESTIMATED
                                              MARKET VALUE

Bank Accounts, Building Society
Deposits etc.
Investments, shareholdings
Family Residence
Second Home
Major Furniture and Furnishings
Caravan, Boat
Vehicle(s)

Hi-fi Equipment
Television, Video Equipment
Appliances (refrigerator, washer, microwave)
Garden Equipment, Power Tools
Garage Equipment
Sports Equipment

Clothing
Linen, Bedding, Floor Coverings
Typewriter, Cameras, Binoculars
Personal Articles of Value
Musical Instruments
Jewellery
Luggage
Other
                              ----

* Cash Value if Sold
   (not original cost)

INVENTORY: THINGS (LIABILITIES)

LIABILITIES   CURRENT STATUS OF
                                         ALL LOANS ETC.

Mortgage
Mortgage on Other Property
Car Loan
Financing Company Loans on Consumer Goods
Credit Outstanding (Visa, Access)
Credit Outstanding (Retail Stores, Mail Order)
Home Improvement Loan
Personal Loans (Family, Friends)

Outstanding Debts for Services Rendered
Borrowings for Investment or Business Purposes
Tax Liabilities Outstanding
Estate Settlements in Trust (Not Disbursed)

Gambling or Betting Debts
Liens on Property Through Bad Debts

Imminent Expenditures Committed or Known

(ASSETS LESS LIABILITIES = NET WORTH)

MONTHLY INCOME & EXPENSES

INCOME   RECEIPTS

Salary, Wages, Commissions from Sales
Part-time Earnings
Second Job
Partner's Employment
Income from Estate Settlement
Alimony, Maintenance, or Other Court Payments
Pension
Income from Former Employers
Social Security Benefits
Unemployment Benefit
Voluntary Payments from Relatives

Bank, Building Society Interest
Investment Income (Share Dividends, Interest)
Rental Income (Property, Other)
Business Income
Other Receipts

EXPENSES   MONTHLY OUTGOINGS

Mortgage, Rent, Rates
Car Expenses, including insurance
Food and Household
Heating, Lighting, Telephone
Maintenance of Property
Insurances
Entertainment and Social Expenses
Miscellaneous Outgoings

(INCOME LESS EXPENSES = NET MONTHLY EXCESS)

Four   Preparing a Personal Inventory

Believe me, the type of person you are is more important than your income or net worth. It is nice to have money and possessions, but if you are poor in personal attributes and qualities, real success will elude you. Even John D. Rockefeller discovered that. It is unlikely that you exist merely to gather more and more possessions, money in the bank, and endless equities around the world. Conversely, there is no call for any negative stigma about material things. In fact, by consuming, you are helping money to move in the economy and hopefully create jobs, directly or indirectly. But, that's right: there has to be more! Personal "things" are just as vital to our sense of well-being and overall prosperity as things we can acquire or buy. In fact, they are a pre-requisite to real success.

What sort of person are you in terms of personal qualities? Do people like you, or are you just fooling yourself about your popularity? It is possible you have areas of difficulty in coping with other people, and yourself. Are you at peace with the world? Is your ego in control of your behaviour, to your detriment?

It was really coming down as John approached the Building Society branch office. The water droplets made his spectacles useless, and he tilted his head around to focus on the door handle. Inside, it was hot as hell. His glasses steamed up at once. He was conscious of the place being mobbed. He collided heavily with a woman's child dangling somewhere below.

He could feel the sweat mingling with the droplets of rain on his face. He felt uncomfortable all over. He was certainly over-dressed for this place; it was stuffy and full of other people's germs. Sneezes, coughs and blowing noses reminded him of the hazards. It was noisy, as people came and went.

After twenty minutes of studying the various communication problems of everyone before him, it was his turn. He stood before the heavy plate glass and said his piece in a discrete, subdued voice. (His business was not for the whole world to hear). The girl mouthed something like "Sorry, I can't...." so he tried again, louder, but closer to the glass. It made no difference.

His voice was too soft to penetrate the glass. It was useless. He passed the books and papers through the sliding trough in the counter. She couldn't understand what he really wanted; it wasn't a cash withdrawal or anything simple. His mind raced ahead.

Why must they isolate us by glass this thick? Why isn't there a speaking hole or something? A microphone? This is ridiculous! It's like an oven in here! Look at those people standing in line, like Polish housewives out for their bread and sausages! This is insane! I want to see the manager! I want to close my account!

The girl watched him as he stood gaping at the sliding trough. *A hole in the counter!* He placed his head down to the trough and began speaking into it. The girl sprung from her chair and withdrew to the back of the office. The lady at the next window also jumped. Robbery in progress! Code 211. Man threatening defenceless women through Building Society counter!

He stood back and glanced at the queue, all the way out to the door now, with two neat zig-zags. They were all frozen with terror, their eyes fixed on his. Taking the floor like Basil Fawlty, he spoke his lines to the assembled audience, loud enough to penetrate the thickest plate glass.

"Have I become Jaws, a giant mouse perhaps, maybe a vicious flea? What? This is the toyshop next door? Oh I see! The wrong shop! Or the optician's? Don't mind me, I've just come to get my brain tested!"

He continued his performance with a complete description of the transactions he wanted to accomplish. His summing-up touched on a vote of thanks to the staff, who must handle all types of absurd people through heavy plate glass every day. The atmosphere was intense; time had stopped. The assembly was transfixed, as if in collective prayer.

If only we could behave like that, have a good laugh, then get our business done! In a sense, the unfettered part of our mind would prefer us to operate in a more open fashion, but we do have a certain social courtesy to maintain in the world. We are expected to behave ourselves in set ways, in each environment. In our city business, at work, in our own homes, travelling on a train, at a job interview, visiting a friend in hospital. It would be fair to say we are different people in our everyday life situations. This has been discussed earlier. Crossing the very rigid boundaries from a socially unprincipled environment to a formal one, carrying badly chosen behaviour over, is usually disastrous. People always mistake inappropriate drama for sarcasm, cynicism, or plain aggression. It is essential to realise that we do have control over ourselves; the trick is to acquire the skill of proving it.

You may not please all the people, all the time. That is an ongoing risk. If we can find ways of relating to *ourselves* in a balanced way, then we are less likely to give little demonstrations at the local Building Society office. It might seem like a jungle out there sometimes, but be sure you are not growing rain-forests and their associated storms inside your head. The dividing line between reason and the ridiculous is often blurred. At times, we miss some excitement or exceptionally good exchanges of humour because we act too stiff and restrained. That is a great pity, but take care where you draw the line between tact and letting go.

Underlying problems, created by bad experiences in the past, often cause us to have strong attitudes, resulting in excessive or irrational outbursts. If you can identify intense experiences that have upset you deeply (or are still doing so), document them on paper. Write out the details, in short story form. Bring out all the nasty things that happened, what people said at the time, and how you felt. Recall your reactions. Were they similar to our friend's in the Building Society, all drama but little real substance or hostility? Until you re-visit and quantify your bad experiences, you will be carrying a heavy load of luggage around with you. *Knowing and understanding* what your problems are, is the essential first step in helping yourself.

Everyone has their own personal world view. This is your position based on your background, everyday situation, your politics, spiritual feelings, how people treat you, your ideas of happiness, and your exposure to news and the interpretation of that. All of us, whatever shortcomings we believe we have in education and experience, have a general philosophy and basic understanding of even the most complex issues.

Your specific perception may not be the same as the person next to you, but the same things affect all people. Nobody has the "right" perception, because we are individually experiencing life under different circumstances. Since our individual world views are also different, the combinations of perception, and our reactions to them, are staggering!

Attitudes give shape to our world view, and our world view gives shape to our attitudes. Be aware of that in every situation you find yourself in. If you are a decided pessimist, based on losing your job twice through redundancies, or losing your matrimonial home to a scheming ex-husband, you may treat a prospective partner in your business with suspicion and underlying contempt. Similarly, that type of person may view any hope of arms reductions among the superpowers as futile and simplistic.

Someone who believes that all people are fundamentally "good", regardless of where they come from, will generally have sensitive and caring attitudes. There will be a common bond with people, whether they are dear old folks getting off a bus, or young hooligans spraying a wall with aerosol cans. Polarised judgements cause separation between people, and we get caught in the games of escalation. That solidifies attitudes and world view, making us excessively narrow-minded (and possibly miserable). Believe that the world is a nasty, selfish, unjust place, and it really will be.

Notwithstanding all this, we like to live our lives around our attitudes and world view. These structural mechanisms allow us to handle the daily process of hearing and seeing information, and dealing with others. Generally, we are surprisingly tolerant. We probably don't get too disturbed if our best friend has the opposite view from us on an issue. We assume that their world view is wrong, or inverted, producing their strange attitudes to things. There is nothing peculiar about having opposing reactions or opinions on the same events or experiences. That is a human foible, worth celebrating rather than condemning. The endless search for truth and absolute values in our lives is a commendable goal, and relies on debate rather than fixed laws. Science is best at claiming and proving truth. But even old time-worn theories get the heave every now and then in favour of better ones. Newtonian science has been challenged by relativity; who will supersede Einstein? *Stop searching for a list of absolutes to fit your life into.* Just accept that there are many ways to describe the same thing, and don't miss the fun because you have *opinions* on everything.

Our ideas on *reality* are also tied in with attitudes and world view. We all have our own circumstances, and these are important to us. Often it is difficult to know what we really do think. Ask someone in the street how their world view translates to their reality!

Usually, we establish contact with reality by noticing things in our routine affairs. We do not intentionally set out each morning, determined to discover what it is that gives us purpose, or makes us add up to a whole person. The process is not that simple. We are not programmed machines with questions, always looking for answers. "What can I expect this year? Why are they treating me like this?" Reality is more than answers to questions. It might be reasonable to assume that we cannot find the answers, because we haven't framed the right questions.

We have to experience life to make any sensible comment on it. Very often, we just have to patiently sit there, letting time go by, until we realise "this is reality for you chum". Your attitudes and world view will determine if the experience is worthwhile or not. But the judgement is relative to you alone. Once we discover our own reality, that doesn't mean we're cornered. We can change our reality.

The road outside is unusually busy today. One inside lane is stopped altogether. People late for meetings are trying to get through. It's windy again;

leaves are finally letting go. Low clouds give the impression the world is moving through space. A strange feeling. Like two trains in a station. Which train is moving?

The traffic is easing. A rusty chimney pipe is stayed by four rusty guy-wires. I can see a heat-haze from it. Two women in the office across the road are exchanging snapshots, laughing; they light up cigarettes. In the next office, their supervisor is picking his nose, looking at Situations Vacant in the Daily Telegraph.

Two lanes are blocked now, in both directions. Probably an accident somewhere. The low cloud seems to have dispersed. The world has slowed down again. It is Tuesday. Another Tuesday. Another year killed in this dreary office.

Is a personal inventory vital to your progress? Well, without it, you may be unaware of flaws in your personality and behaviour that limit your potential. We tend to suppress our personal shortcomings because we know there's a lot of pain involved when we disturb the murky waters deep inside us. Unfortunately, we don't know how to identify and measure the qualities we have, or do not have. You can count money on a table and write down the total. You can list the denominations and the dates on the coins. If you're a history enthusiast, you can even trace the events that the money on your table witnessed. Can you count your *personal worth* and embellish it with facts in the same way? It is extremely difficult to be open about our personal strengths and weaknesses. We fluctuate between flushes of ego (the good qualities) and torment (the real nasties). Be honest with yourself. Your personal inventory is a mixture of some good personal traits, some you know could be better, and a set that you may attribute to a hostile demon lodged deep inside you.

You are well aware that material success alone is shallow and unsatisfying without personal qualities you are proud of. You want to *feel* good when you count your money! People that come into your life want to feel that you are a decent person, unlikely to plot against them, or let them down because you are forgetful and indecisive. What you are aiming for is a material-personal combination that will *expand your reality, and as you circulate, expand the possibilities of your world.*

The first thing is to get something down on paper. Once we commit thoughts and facts to paper, we start to establish contact with ourselves. You did it for your Financial Inventory. Counting money was relatively easy, wasn't it? Use a pencil and have an eraser standing by. You will make lots of mistakes! But don't erase the truth about yourself. You are not going to share your worksheets with anyone. So that gives you freedom to open up. Before proceeding with the interrogation, write a short autobiography in 400 words. Start with your childhood and work forward. Pace it out so that your last ten years get about 60% of the words. Your story should include facets of your education, family life, major relationships, outline of work history (but not a CV), interests, type of person you think you are, and a statement about your immediate situation, dilemma, crossroads, or whatever.

Review what you have written, and ask yourself if you are on the mark, or if it looks like sugary self-inflation. Are *you really in* that autobiography? Take the time now to revise it and cut out useless facts about how well you handled that interview five years ago, or the waffle about archery changing your world view.

Now. Consider the following list of prompts to help you draw a reasonably comprehensive sketch of yourself. No need to write out the list; just concentrate on the answers. Take an interest in this; you are trying to communicate with yourself. If you don't think it's worth the time or effort, then you are essentially denying yourself a chance to grow.

PERSONAL REVIEW

1. Personal Attributes

Are you imaginative? Can you see most problems with a fresh outlook and come up with smart ideas?

Are you self-confident in the sense of being able to handle any situation without going to pieces?

How persistent are you in getting things done, even if it's an uphill struggle?

Do you assume responsibilities easily and happily?

Are you courteous to people at all times, in all situations?

How independent are you (functioning alone)?
Do you make decisions objectively or subjectively?

Are you a good communicator, written, oral?

Do you deal with people in a mature way, allowing for the range of human differences?

How rigid are you about your opinions and alignments when discussing things with other people? Are you willing to accept the other viewpoint?

How developed is your intuition and sensitivity to things that are not said or communicated by normal means?

Do you consider yourself good at your job, even if you are not entirely satisfied with it?

How assertive do you think you are?

Do you adapt quickly to change and move on from there?

2. Interpersonal Maturity

Do you gain trust and respect from people with relative ease?

Are you willing to listen for extended periods without giving your point of view?

Can you win people's confidence and then willingly form a team around you to solve a problem?

Do you find it difficult meeting new people: in a work environment; socially?

When an argument develops into a row, do you continue to its conclusion, or find a way of escaping? Can you moderate your own anger?

Are you insecure in your relationship with your partner, or family members?
Does the public showing of affection, to family or strangers, cause you discomfort?

Do you honestly forgive people who rub you the wrong way?

How patient are you?

Do you get worked up and very "involved" by news items or controversial topics of conversation?

Are you anxious about making a good impression in all situations, including home life? Do you see life as a competitive game?

How open-minded are you when faced with unusual viewpoints or unfamiliar lifestyles?

3. List the skills you have, without restricting yourself to past or present work experience. Dealing effectively with people is a skill; so is building ornamental rabbit hutches.

4. List any special skills, or unique talents (amateur tree-doctor, closet poetry writing, retouching old photographs, special rapport with young children or restless youth).

5. What things in life give you the most *lasting and satisfying* returns? This is wide open. Bringing up children, splitting atoms in a linear accelerator, pigeon fancying, climbing the career ladder by sheer effort, spending money on wild sprees, travelling to unlikely places, discovering your higher purposes, building a special relationship.

6. Direction

Is your life useful at present? In what ways?

Do you accept that certain things about you could be changed for the better, if you really wanted?

How do you feel about risk?
Do you believe that you are in control of your life, rather than being subject to every negative development from the external environment?

Does the idea of being ambitious upset your desire for security?

How much do you think your background influences what you feel now, and what you will experience and achieve in the future?

Do you make decisions routinely and easily, or anguish over them?

Do you think that making a plan for the future is futile, even if you know what you basically want?

Which direction do you feel you are going in at present? Is it a path of total stagnation and despair; a haven of stability and sufficiency; or one that offers some growth, maybe some real changes for the better?

How cynical a person are you regarding the process of learning and applying feedback on yourself? Are you above all that?

The sad part about this exercise: there is no list of right answers! But did you have any interesting thoughts and feelings during your probing? It would be nice to have a snappy little checklist to see how unbalanced or unsatisfactory we are! However, only you can set standards: you will know where you would like to be. Record these ideas for future reference.

It takes effort to build up a picture of you. The medium of this book can only prompt you to open up to yourself. If you are wanting to progress, be willing to put in some work. Consider the skills you listed. Did you learn them at a single sitting? The Personal Review exercise gives you the chance, in the privacy of your own space, to construct a reasonable image of yourself. These notes are your notes. If they are honest and to the point, you are serious about yourself. If not, give yourself a second chance and apply yourself more diligently. It will pay off in the end.

The wonderful thing about humans: they have certain acquired faculties built-in that help to quantify things. Our eyes and our brain work together to warn us that a car cannot be driven through a space one inch too narrow. We can scrape the car in somehow, but that means ignoring our inner signals. Similarly, we know very quickly if we have offended someone or lost their trust. We read letters from partners, lovers, children, parents and friends. The words don't say it all. We *know* that there's something not quite right. Between the lines, or in the tone and choice of words, it's there alright. You have just finished answering some questions, and presumably, you have made the effort to do your best and be honest. Read your notes. Read between the lines. Add facts and feelings you missed. Give your exercise life, and understand what it is saying to you. Then summarise your thoughts on the matter.

To help you to imagine what an all-round balanced person might look like, some attributes and qualities are listed for you. The list can never be complete, because each of us perceives "good" qualities to be relative to "bad" ones, and relative to our individual preferences. For example, honesty is often a relative thing. We all manipulate this loophole to suit everyday requirements, some more than others of course. (Does your boss realise all this study is preparing you for your *next* job?). The practice of elasticity in terms of honesty does not imply that absolute truth is a myth. Our society places demands on us regarding truth. For instance, withholding information is seen as par for the course, if releasing it might harm others. Too much of this may cause actual lying, however. Examine the personal attributes and qualities with wisdom. There may be other shades of grey.

COMMONLY RECOGNISED PERSONAL ATTRIBUTES AND QUALITIES

Honesty
Compassion
Patience
Focus   Lose focus, and your mind is everywhere.
Self Respect   Why should I put myself down?
Cheerfulness   Life is tough, but don't drag us all down.
Attitude   You *can* get there from here.
Will-power
Originality
Resourcefulness
Strength   Weakness leads to weakness.
Perseverance
Curiosity   You never know enough. Stay interested.
Innovation
Sincerity   People are helpful to open, faithful folk.
Vitality   This is the celebration of life.
Communication
Sensitivity
Feeling
Decisiveness   Procrastination achieves mediocrity.
Wisdom

Vision	Dreamers are the ones to watch.
Ability	There must be *something* we can do well.
Order	A tidy mind can find what's required.
Disposition	
Maturity	
Peace	Conflict is all around. Stay cool.
Effectiveness	
Confidence	Without this and you can't face yourself.

After perusing the list of personal qualities, you might now have a picture of where you are, and where you might like to be. There are no prizes or reprimands for your situation. The key is to recognise the progress you made. Compliment yourself; you are doing nicely.

The self-image you have constructed over the years may not be entirely to your satisfaction. Over your lifetime to date, you have assembled many experiences and your perception of them. People have told you how pathetic you are, or what a complete mess you made of something. Parents and teachers are skilled in it. You may have built or drawn something as a child, only to experience laughter, which you took to be disapproval. Perhaps you completed a particularly difficult project at school or work, something you felt was a breakthrough and a joy to behold. Some authority figure then proceeded to criticise your project, until there seemed to be no useful purpose in even explaining the good points. Negative childhood experiences are particularly damaging and often produce severe (but well masked) transference problems for the adult self-image. We are all affected somewhat by this, all candidates for some interesting analysis!

These harmful experiences are real. They happen, and they hurt our pride at any stage of our lives. We are usually in a position of weakness at the time, which makes the painful business more penetrating. "That's the last time I help *that* demanding clown" you say. Then you move on to more bad experiences and the pattern is set to say "I don't help anyone now; they don't deserve it". Some of us are more sensitive to those affairs than others. Very often, the sensitive ones are the most creative in the first place, and their individual achievement is thwarted by the stupid comments of fools. It is a tragedy of human nature and to some extent we do it to each other all the time. The real tragedy lies in the strong residual damage to our self-image. Those with thick skins move on to the next project, oblivious of the damage inflicted by the last one. How many of us have those thick skins? Very few, when it comes right down to it. Many hours of psychotherapy are spent finding the causes of neuroses. Far too many neuroses stem from long forgotten damage to the self-image system.

When past experience or distorted ideas about ourselves harms our present and our future, we *must consciously rebuild our self-image as quickly as possible.* Self-image governs your attitudes to everything you experience or do. When a person believes they are worthless, clumsy, shy, introverted, and generally short of the mark, performance in everything obeys the negative image. Shy people, for example, stare at the floor and wring their hands; as they speak, their breathing is short, shallow, and confused with the actual words coming out. Since self-image governs the proceedings, all the added extras like blushing, sweating, eye evasion and foot games reinforce the overall picture. "See, I'm shy. You can tell, can't you? Just look at my contorted facial muscles and feel my clammy hands!" You are not a failure! Who told you that? Well, they were wrong! You are learning to understand your attributes, your shortages, and what may be lurking in the shadows. Decide what is important for you, and be certain that yesterday has indeed gone. You can *do something* about those personal shortages, other than worrying over them and bending your life to fit a pattern which is less than you deserve.

Part II

Where do you want to be, in spite of everything?

"Oh, I know what I want. That's easy. But getting it, ah well...."

"I wish I was someone interesting; I'm pretty dull really".

"Honestly, I don't know what I want out of life, not when I think deeply about it".

"I've always found that life gives you what's coming to you. What *I'd like* doesn't come into it at all".

"The way the world's going, you're lucky to survive at all. Asking more than that is ridiculous".

Five   What Do You Want?

You have now roughly established what material things and personal attributes you have. It is unlikely you are totally satisfied, whatever inventories you present. Already the panic might be rising in you, when you reflect on how little you seem to have, or the emphasis you have uncovered. Asking someone what they want, appears to be one of the simplest questions, whether it is directed to an adult or a child. But the problem lies with specifics, and that is far from simple.

In fact, it might be the hardest thing of all to define what you want. It might even be harder than actually setting out to *get* what you want. How do we know our own mind and what it really wants for us (if that is actually where *wanting* originates)? Is it the mind we must look to when preparing our list of wants?

Honesty comes into play, and this is inseparable from a developed sense of openness. It is vital that you end up with the right things, otherwise you will be chasing clouds in a thunderstorm. You alone can define what things you want in your life. The external world will be useless to you in that search. So don't start looking for your inspiration or guidance from popular trends, or well-researched features in The Economist. Enjoy your involvement with the external world, for that is where you operate right now. But don't let your environment or your circumstances dictate what comes first, second or last in your life. If you are an Open Person, you will *know* why you want certain things.

Children are impossible when it comes to what they want. A great deal can be learned from their little lives and how their realities function. Take two children to a large department store on the second last Saturday before Christmas! Their minds are busy, to say the least. What you see is a study of human behaviour, in miniature, but superbly focused. Their limited attention span prohibits them from making constructive proposals on what they really want. Each moment leads to a new moment, as it should. The kids buzz around from toy to toy, from games to pink rabbits to computers. Their little thoughts are directed at the fulfilment of big desires. Money doesn't come into this scenario! As we explain limitations (lack of money, items too big or too old for them, poor quality), the children get cranky. There's nothing worse than kids whining their dissatisfaction about limited resources (amidst abundance) in your tired ears!

Of course, as we get older, we supposedly get wiser. We hopefully begin to realise that things we accumulate, like toys in our childhood, do not bring with them lasting joy and contentment. A car is nice, but it will rust and it will give us problems and headaches once the big ends go. It is a fact of life that material things will one day leave our lives, even if it is only when we die. The whole business of insurance is indirectly linked to the myth that we can sustain everything, if we only pay a premium to some nice man that calls at our house on Monday evenings.

Don't be fooled by your mind, however well-intentioned it appears. Your mind is pre-occupied trying to sort your affairs out; it sends little messages to the you that's in there somewhere. Its dialogue might be:

"Look, I'm doing my best to get you all I think you want, but things are tough in here. Besides, you don't help me too much. So, I'll teach you a lesson. I'll make you miserable because you're not getting all I think you should have. So miserable you'll be convinced you're a failure. Confused? Well, serves you right. I'm whacked doing all your thinking and wanting for you, and even more whacked worrying for you about things not working out!"

You just can't win! Perhaps your lively, constructive mind comes up with a generous thought like: "I think it's time this poor soul was made a partner in the firm". Somehow, the partnership doesn't materialise. How will your mind react to the bad news? "You're a failure; there's a conspiracy going on, let's track it down; life is unfair, unjust, show them your anger". Your mind works overtime to substantiate and justify every angle, cast up every frustrated dream. This all seems abstract, but *listening to the dialogue of your mind can lead you a merry chase.* Thoughts, feelings and desires all go off like fireworks thrown on a bonfire; no warnings, no apparent reason or order.

There is a hollowness in simply wanting for wanting's sake. Consider the children. You might buy them every single thing their little minds told them they "wanted". Their little minds would be studying (and wanting) even more things, while the first load of items was being wrapped! Ask for their updated list of wants one week later. It will be as long as ever. Novelty will have worn thin, and the relentless search for gratification will wind itself up for more.

Our unfocused minds alone are unreliable guides in the formulation of realistic "want plans". That is why we are not rushing into jotting down your goals, so you can be quickly on your way to creating your own personal want list. Your mind sometimes says you are hungry, after you've polished off a fine dinner and the leftovers. Do you stuff more food down your gullet? Just because your mind says "You're hungry you old slob, get eating"? Your mind makes you jump out of your skin when something goes bump in the night. Is there always imminent danger threatening you?

Treat your mind with respect. They don't do brain transplants yet, so be kind to it. Your mind really is the marvel they all say it is, better than any computer around. Nevertheless, be careful about its limitations and its *modus operandi*. By itself, it cannot give you the vision to set up what you really want from life. It's not that type of instrument. You can't find a ship's position with a compass; you use a sextant. Heading alone is meaningless, if you don't know where you are coming from. Are we going East to Panama or East to Penzance?

Wanting is like breathing or sneezing. Wanting is like a cat stealing your sausages just because you left them lying there. No other reason! You see a nice dress; you want it. (If you never saw it, would you want it?). You spot a charming cottage in Oxford; you want it. You hear there's work in Los Angeles at McDonnell Douglas; you want it. There's cheap furniture at a liquidation sale; you want some. Your friend in Liverpool has a programmable microwave; you must have one. There's reduced fares to the Far East; you want a ticket. Your sister has interesting friends; you want some too. Your brother wants you over to see the Calgary Stampede; you want to go. You go there; you want to emigrate!

Your mind is looking after you in the best way it knows. Give it credit where it is due. When presented with a sequence of possibilities, your mind is indeed a wonder. For example, after a holiday somewhere, you decide you would like to live there. Perhaps you had a vague dissatisfaction with your former location, but this grows to total disgust, now you think you smell greener grass. The mind wants what it thinks is best for you, then works with you to get the details sorted out. The ultimate process of moving to the new place is handled by the conscious, ever-so-logical mind. Finding ways to finance everything, selling up the old place, and establishing work at the new, are all juggled and executed by the mind. What else?

Before we get into the serious business of determining what you really want, and what success means to you, take time to consider the strange anomalies of the mind. There is nothing to be gained by quickly writing up a list of wants, then posting it up the magic chimney of your mind. Your mind will agree with your list without question. (It's short-circuited by wants wanted, and wants frustrated, remember?). But rather than trying to drive you into a chicken-and-egg, or, "where-have-I-put-my-mind" spiral, let's move on to more fruitful things. Take your mind along. It's welcome. But keep your eye on it. It can be a tricky and unreliable piece of machinery!

Discover for yourself at the outset, a means of detaching the popular stereotypes of "success" from what you feel to be right for you. That is a sincere but loaded requisition. Do you really want a Porsche, or do you really hate driving altogether, no matter what image the wheels carry? Do you emphatically believe that success lies in a better job? Or are you more realistically the type of person who could be in ecstasy on a low income, pottering at a lovely hobby you have? Do you feel that you are pushing yourself to make more and more friends, when you are actually happier with a small group of close confidantes? Is it necessary for you to uproot yourself to make a fresh start, or could you sort things out where you are, and perhaps feel more content in the long run?

The *future of success itself* is interesting, and worth commenting upon right at the start. Popular models of success are slowly changing, so be aware of that. Money is becoming less central to the fabric of real success (ignore the clever Dicks who gloat about turning over their house for a small fortune). The successful people in the future might be those who:

-Are increasingly independent of all the usual constraints (job, mortgage, living on credit, gathering possessions just to be in the game).
-Desire wholeness rather than novelty. They know that money does not buy happiness or fulfilment, but use money as leverage to create the things that do.

-Understand "the system" for what it is. The system needs large numbers of competitive people, to nourish and perpetuate itself. Those who feel the system is really all there is, will continue to be slaves to it and be strangers to themselves. Their arbitrary ideas of success will lead them round in circles. To earn a good salary, one must live in expensive cities. To compete in style, one must accept debt and seek a higher salary. So it goes on. It's hard to think clearly when part of the rat race.

-Return to a simpler world view and enjoy pleasures long forgotten. Rather than seeking oblivion from the present through the pleasure-principle, they will be learning how to grow beautiful flowers. Or taking music lessons instead of renting videos or listening to formula heavy metal.

-Appreciate quality in everything. Rather than buying shoddy (but trendy) mass-produced goods, they will seek well made (even home-made) articles that last and can be repaired.

-Instead of blaming everything (the government, banks, stock market, economy, recessions, parents, weather), will be using their own inner resources to create success. And *success that they really do want, not the success that people crave under the present consensus.* You are not a failure if you don't want a personal helicopter, or a 10,000 square foot house. Trying to pursue goals that society specifies is absurd!

What we perceive to be success and what we think we must do to get some of the action, might both be mistakes from the start. That is why I am labouring over this. Does success mean driving around your old neighbourhood in a Rolls-Royce, giving the neighbours the look-at-me treatment? Is success jetting around on business, being interviewed by the top journals? You name it! But there is no need to copy anyone else just because you're short of ideas yourself. You can be original with your success. Too many people are copycats. That, in a way, is cloning of the imagination. It is a waste of human talent and energy.

When we moved into our new house, most of our neighbours were like ourselves. Married one or two years with a child, one on the way, or thinking about it. It was a new development. The streets were still muddy from the builders. It was a new start for us after renting a dismal flat. Our expectations were high.

We joined forces with the neighbours; building fences, moving earth about, buying materials together. That summer was tiring, but fun. We became close through our labours, enjoying many pots of tea and shared laughter.

I think our problems began with the parties. At first, they were simple affairs, an extension of our moving-in chumminess. A round of parties seemed a good way to house-warm our little community. Each party was slightly more grand than the last. It was imperceivable at first, but the pattern was established by the sixth. We survived the first round, but it wiped out our money for a tumble dryer. The second round was not so easy.

Then we fell in with Len and Phyllis. They dined out in style once a week; Phyllis called it their weekly reward. We couldn't say no, so we dined with them. Dave next door convinced us we should have a better car; he had a friend in the trade. So we got a new car. It looked great in our drive. We signed up an expensive life insurance policy (that was Bill, two doors away). Then Mary suggested we join their group for a skiing holiday in France over the Christmas period. It was all very exciting, and we knew it was good to have really close neighbours that helped us all the time.

Within six months we were broke. Our bank account and the loan from dad were history. The car was repossessed. When the furniture was lifted, our neighbours kept away. In fact, we haven't seen them since.

Now we live with my parents, but it's a squeeze. The house sold again, to a nice young couple like us. We walked past one evening, about 8.30. There was music from our house. A new car stood in the drive, with a ski-rack on the roof. Through the lace curtains, we noticed Bill explaining insurance numbers on his calculator; Len and Phyllis were explaining the tasting of wine.

Smiling at each other, we walked on to the chip-shop and ordered suppers with double pickled onions. We ate them on the way to the bus stop, just as we did when we first met, staring up in wonder at our own special stars.

The truth is, many people haven't a clue what they want, but they keep their minds actively "wanting" all the while, unwittingly drawing disappointment upon themselves. "Don't know specifically what I want, so I'll be miserable meanwhile!" The energy spent wanting is spread so thin, that legitimate wants are seldom realised. If the energy was applied to one or two meaningful goals, with a vision of attainment, life might be less frustrating. You might not have much, but be thankful for it. Everything you have, whether it's a tank of tropical fish or the ability to make people laugh at the pub, be thankful for it. If you are miserable with what you have now, what logic says you are going to be a joyful person when you have possessions stacked to the roof? Many people have not progressed much beyond the example of the children in the toy department. It is fruitless to gather things around you in the vague hope that some synergy will occur, spawning instant happiness. Only if they are the *right things* will this occur.

The young couple did what was expected of them, and at the time, they had no idea what path they *should* have been on. We cannot glibly say they were silly to be led by others, and deserved to fall.

They acted in good faith at the time. How many young couples in the first flush of partnership sit down and draw up a life-map to follow? In their case, they were convinced they were making progress in the right place at the right time. (With so many sincere neighbours about them to help, of course). They had no final option but to withdraw from the dizzy race and return to reality, which essentially meant nothing more than living within their means. It is a sad thing when we must withdraw because of external circumstances, and not through conscious choice. But the lessons learned are valuable, if we can accept them graciously rather than with a feeling of devastation. The couple seemed relieved to be out of the game, eating their chips and counting the stars. Was the wanting game as tempting to them now as it had been before? Did they pound on their heads with little hammers? "You failed, you failed, you failed, and everyone's laughing at you!" Fortunately, they survived rather well. It is clear they have set yesterday where it belongs; their immediate goal is to finish their pickled onions before going on the bus.

Change is the best example of a universal truth we can honestly accept without much protest. You buy a house; you sell it. You get a job; you change it. You have a partner; you lose your partner. You buy shares; the prices go up. You place money in floating bonds; the rate plummets. The hairdresser quits; you have to adjust to the mysterious Antoine. As change manifests itself in so many dimensions of our lives, our needs change. Our family is growing; we need a bigger house. The job is more demanding; we need a company car. The job is lost; we need to cut expenses and scan the adverts.

When change arrives, we seldom consciously insist on choices that suit us personally. For example, from experience, we believe that by not accepting a promotion, we won't ever be shortlisted for good positions in the future. So we do as we are told, in effect. Change is king in a world of change. When we are offered opportunities, we can view them in three distinct ways. First: God this is awful, I'll hate this from the start, but it's a good leg up after all; I'll take it and the extra cash. Second: This is the very opportunity I've been dreaming of; I feel better already. Third: This is not for me. It will only set me back when I take my personal goals into account. It sounds like a good chance for someone, but not me.

Which candidate are you? Number three is taking a risk experimenting with his or her future like this. It could be the last available rung of the ladder. The powers-that-be may treat this person like an ungrateful wretch, and poison the working environment. So the individualist withdraws and disappears; a rejected failure in the eyes of peers and observers.

How do you see it? We ought to believe in our judgement and stick to our resolution. If a prospect is really not for you, seek an alternative. You might end up getting *something that appears worthwhile, but did you originally want it?* Life is full of choices if you could but generate and exploit them. There is no such thing as "I must" when it comes to others (or your own vain mind) forcing you into choices. Follow your nose, as they say. It might make more sense than pursuing comfortable but unsatisfying oblivion. Real alternatives are your fundamental human rights. Don't say you are trapped; you are always able to find alternatives, but show a little patience.

I was new to Calgary, and I took an apartment near the Bow River. One Saturday evening, I felt it would be nice to know someone and go out to a movie or something. It wasn't likely to suddenly happen, so I put the supper on and strolled out to my balcony, nineteen floors up.

Across the street, and across an open parking lot, stood the twin towers of the trendiest place to have an apartment in Calgary. I noticed a lovely girl leaning on the railing, perhaps twenty-two floors up. She looked around and studied the taxicabs and night traffic on the way to good times. I wished at that moment she could be with me to share my steak and onions.

Between looking over at her, and turning my steak over, forty minutes passed. I could see her, but I realised she was totally unaware of me.

I sat down to my supper. The noise of the city streamed in through my open patio door. Police cars chased around, sirens blooping on and off to give speedsters tickets. One siren whined away. A fire truck maybe. It stopped somewhere down below. Living in a high-rise apartment, people always check out where the fire truck stops.

It wasn't a fire truck, but an ambulance and two police cars, blocking two lanes on Sixth Avenue. I picked out a red blanket on the street, then the form of a person. A pedestrian hit by a car. I looked up at the apartment opposite. People were standing there, spectating from their balconies. I wondered why the girl wasn't there, because her patio door was open. Then it all clicked.

She was wearing the same blue-green dress and a necktie. There was no red blanket; they were putting sand down on it now. The ambulance pulled away; the siren was not used.

It made no news. I found out the details from a friend at work who stayed in the same apartment block. She had broken up with her boyfriend of two months, because he was going to college down East in Toronto. Twenty. A Saturday night in Calgary, Houston of the Great White North, with absolutely no alternatives.

Are you a special person, or are you ordinary? Let's play risky and say you are extra special. It does not mean you are better, of course. That is a subjective game of nonsense. When you believe that you are special, you will help others to realise they might be special too.

Every special person has special needs. Special people have very special ideas of what they're here for, and what they're going to make of it all. They assimilate with their own unique properties and hidden potential. They understand and learn to have control over what is going on, rather than blindly accepting what is presented to them. By understanding themselves well, and appreciating how this funny old world (against all the odds) continues to carry on every day, they discover things about life they once thought must be secret. These are the hidden secrets kept from mankind, by mankind.

Special people learn how to identify and align themselves with the things they want. They refuse to model every thinking moment on other people's lives, or the complications thereof. They refuse to compare what they have or do not have with neighbours, friends, or characters in the media (or fantasy). Special people refuse to forfeit their hard-won contentment and peace of mind, when put under pressure from the fanatical ideas of others. They refuse to allow conflict between their inner satisfaction, and the popular consensus about forever wanting more and expecting it to come like manna from heaven.

Your personal wants might appear very straightforward to some people. Perhaps you want nothing. Perhaps you want a chain of international hotels around the world, and a personal 727 to visit them with. Don't feel guilty either way. You are *both* absolutely on target, *if that is what you want!* Your wants can seldom be too simple, or too outrageous. Providence is not going to punish you for appearing greedy. If you set out to get what you want honestly, and it is precisely what you have dedicated your wishes to, then you will *actually get support from Providence!* Disbelieve this at your peril. You don't have all the answers; why are you reading this book?

Jean sent the coupon away, with her choices in order: DGFACEB. She wasn't sure if floor organisation was better than piped music, but that was her choice.

When the letter arrived, she nearly threw it in her coupon box on top of the fridge. Opening it, she discovered she had won first prize: five minutes of fully paid shopping in a giant supermarket.

She picked a Wednesday morning for the spree. Needless to say, she hadn't slept for excitement the night before, and her nerves were getting the better of her for weeks. The manager welcomed her, and the staff were lined up like Upstairs Downstairs. TV and the press were there to follow the event.

After some preliminaries, the clock was started. Jean sped off down the first aisle with the multitude trying to keep up. They couldn't catch her. "She must know what's the best to go for!" they screamed.

She had vanished. Jean was like a rabbit; drawing the pension had nothing to do with it!

A full minute before the timer went off, Jean appeared at checkout 16 with a trolley loaded like a ten-armed man at a looting. Within seconds, everyone was crowded around, TV camera shooting it all.

"I always wanted the very best, but I couldn't afford it. And I hate the carrying. This'll keep me going my lifetime", she said.

Piled on the trolley, like neatly-laid bricks in a master-mason's wall, were 424 best quality toilet rolls, absolutely top-of-the-line and undoubtedly used by the very best.

Preferences

This exercise helps to highlight your *present* tastes. Avoid any structuring: allow free association of ideas. Use the format responses as a prompt.

LIKES
Cheerful people. Learning new things, but not too demanding. Driving my friend's car. Relaxed times with best friends. Non-competitive sports (swimming, hill-walking, cycling). Living in a big city. Weekends and evenings when I can do what I want. Holidays. Well-behaved children. Hot sunny weather. Healthy foods. Feeling fit. Being around smart people who are going somewhere. Having parents that don't preach. Good quality clothes. Writing long letters to old friends. Reading my daily horoscope. Visiting zoos and wildlife parks. Giving my neighbour a lift on wet days. Helping my brother with his business book-keeping. Dreaming about my football pools netting me a small fortune! Working hard at things I enjoy. Responsibilities I can cope with.

DISLIKES
Waiting in queues too long (impatience). People that snub me or put me down. Limitations of present job, in scope and earnings. My car stalling in heavy traffic. Meeting new people. Eating foreign foods or strange dishes in restaurants. Having to do correspondence courses for work. Dogs that bark and snarl at me. British winters. Violent films. People less intelligent than me. Household chores and dull, routine things. Going back to my home town (it's dull). Stuffy people, very rigid ideas. Litter everywhere, dogs' dirt. Underpasses and narrow streets. Arrogant people that never listen to my opinions. Snobbish people that remind me how little I have. Selfish, inconsiderate drivers. Feeling of drifting along at the moment. Critical people, even those thinking they're helping.

This person appears very selective, especially with people. There is a vague desire to be successful, but a lack of interest in applying effort. Although the desire is to be among the "right" things and people, there are signs of holding back, fear of being hurt, and lack of adventure. An essentially kind person, but closed to possibilities beyond safe boundaries. There is evidence of wishing the right "luck" to come along. But the person is unable to accept the responsibility of taking an active part in trying alternatives.

How would *you* describe this person? When you prepare your own "Preferences" worksheet, how would you describe yourself? Sometimes the little things suggest significant patterns of alignment. You might discover your own dislikes fill the page: that might tell you something! If you follow the advice on applying free association to your worksheet, you will notice how willing your mind is to supply you with a wide spectrum of information.

When it comes to applying the outcome of "Preferences", listening to your mind's constant chattering will give you nothing but a jumble of things for you to want. That has been established earlier, to your great confusion no doubt. We need to explore further.

The cheapest and most functional exploration method is a pad of paper, a pencil, an eraser, and a selection of coloured pencils. Then a comfortable, quiet place to sit. You'll need a table or a desk. Sitting in an armchair, with a glass of beer, potato crisps, and the television on, is not the way. So get to it, and organise yourself for a little effort!

Do you know how to "open up" yet on paper? You can learn to use written, graphic and visual techniques to communicate with yourself. Sitting *thinking about your ideas is next to useless,* because your mind has no focus of its own. A mind without focus is like a slide show with the projector lens missing. Don't make things difficult for yourself. The mind is a marvellous tool, but we have to learn how to use it. Computers are also astounding in their own way. But until you press the right buttons, they're a heap of silicon and plastic. Write down ideas, fears, frustrations, dreams, problems. Draw little cartoons or symbols that give you a visual image of how things really are. If you think you're a failure and the world's against you, write all your negative words down. When you see them on paper, you'll begin to realise that perhaps there's still hope. It's good fun. I call it notepad prayer: getting to know yourself, "talking to yourself", in your own everyday words, four-letter ones too if it helps.

Together, we are going to construct a map of your present position and the possibilities open to you. The chart will cover the things that matter at this stage. (You may want to adjust the exercise to your own special needs). Insert key statements in your circular chart after completing the self-assessment. The objective is to get you in touch with yourself, and to help you *extend yourself in the ways you choose*. What you want will hopefully become clear to you as the process develops. If you try to by-pass the exercise and go straight to the "want" level, you'll miss the point. The aim is to determine what is right for you; not just a string of things that seem better than what you presently have.

You will refer to your inventories, already prepared. These exercises helped you to see where you stand, in a relatively quantitative way. Now you will extend these findings into a series of "paper dialogues". Apply the principle of free association of ideas. Don't miss out anything just because it doesn't seem to fit the categories. And keep focused on the task at hand. One step at a time, or you'll end up with an electrical storm in your head. An example chart is built up around a fictitious soul with a realistic situation. Again, use the method, not the similarities.

LEVEL I: FACTS

CIRCUMSTANCES
Living in a two-bedroomed house in Kingston-upon-Thames. Heavy commitments to family and various debts. Job a bit uncertain in the long term (recent layoff). Wife pregnant. Relatives from Yorkshire arriving for holiday this summer. Trying to help brother-in-law find a job in the South.

FINANCES
House value £74,000. Mortgage £58,000. Equity £16,000.
Bank account £7,400.
Bank loan for car £3200 still outstanding.
Possessions, estimated value £2,600. Car £3,400.
Present salary £10,200 pa.

CAREER
Work unstable since recent takeover. Some layoffs already.
New boss difficult to work with.
Generally satisfied with work, but company has changed.
Wife finished part-time work due to baby.
My skills are difficult to apply in other work.

PERSONAL
I can't make decisions any more. I can't concentrate.
I have trouble trusting people now. I look for their faults.
I lose my cool often and let people know what I think.
Recently, I'm tired all the time, lazy and careless.
I'm impatient, ultra-sensitive and lacking daily confidence.

RELATIONSHIPS
Wife is becoming moody and dissatisfied with our lot.
I have quarrels with people at work.
I've lost my faith in people I formerly trusted.
I'm tired of seeing my soccer friends every Friday before a game.

CONSCIOUSNESS
Sometimes I'm "observing" myself, watching my stupid behaviour.
I think people see that I'm not too bright these days.
I have a sense of impending failure when I think too much.
I borrow books on psychology from the local library!

LEVEL II: FEELINGS

CIRCUMSTANCES
I wanted a decent salary after working up North, so here I am. But the mortgage is frightening, with another child on the way. And this damned job! Will I be the next one to get the boot? I wish our relatives would leave the holiday till we get on our feet here. And Linda's brother isn't worth finding a job for!

FINANCES
On paper I'm worth about £20,000 clear. My salary is OK but it could be higher. Up North I'd feel well-off; but I'd have no job. If I lose my job here, the whole thing falls apart. The roof and chimney need maintenance. We're saving nothing now that Linda's stopped work.

CAREER
I'm wary of this firm, especially after the takeover. Sooner or later I'll quit on the spot, because of that clown they put over me. I know all about plastic insulators for electrical appliances, but who else would need that? I painted myself into a bloody corner this time.

PERSONAL
I think I'm falling apart every day. I nearly slapped the wife yesterday, something I swore I'd never do. Every time I try to see a better way, I lose interest and want to sleep in a chair. I just feel I've reached the point of no solutions. I can't think straight.

RELATIONSHIPS
My poor wife! I lie in bed thinking what stupid things I said to her, and I feel remorse to the core. But do I learn? I give her nothing but bickering the next day. My friends seem distant to me. To be honest, I don't have a close friend just now. That's a bad sign!

CONSCIOUSNESS
I'm conscious of being in trouble, or at least out of control. Maybe work isn't altogether to blame. After all, it's not everything. I have nothing substantial to hang onto. My wife, yes, but she thinks I'm on the way down or something. She doesn't say much. The idea of slipping into depression crossed my mind.

LEVEL III: WANTS

CIRCUMSTANCES
We like our house. With two children it will do until an extension
could be added. Other people have high mortgages; ours isn't too
ridiculous. We'll make it clear that our guests pay their way. Tell
Linda's brother to get down here and look for jobs himself!

FINANCES
We're not that badly placed after a year here. If we had to move, we
have enough to manage. The roof hasn't leaked yet, so we can defer
that job. We must have more income with another mouth to feed
soon.

CAREER
I'll start thinking about other jobs that I could use my skills in. Electrical insulators must be used in other things. Maybe magazines
would get me thinking. There's no doubt, I'm not happy with this
firm any more. I'll wait a month or two and ask for a decent salary
rise. Meanwhile, I'll look around.

PERSONAL
My behaviour has to improve. I'll lose my job whether I want to or
not, and my wife will leave me. It's time I developed new interests:
I'm going quite stale. I'm tired of the soccer club; besides, I'm
getting past the game of downing six pints. No more sitting in chairs
and snoozing either!

RELATIONSHIPS
I have to discuss the problems with my wife, rather than brooding
about them myself. She keeps quiet because she's becoming scared of
me! Imagine! I should think about making friends in some new
activity, like a do-it-yourself club. I must find some close friends.
How about my wife, for one?

CONSCIOUSNESS
There's something wrong alright. That's the easy part. I must see it
as it is, and take steps to get out of this hole. I'm more miserable than
I need be: even I can admit to that. Once we get things under way in
the next few months, it will fall into place. Why should I punish
myself and everyone around me?

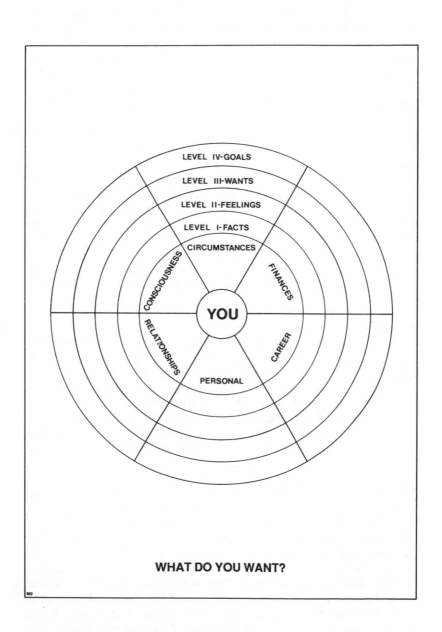

WHAT DO YOU WANT?

Stretching for what we would like, beyond what we have to get along with, is the next step in the proceedings. The case study, designed to help you in *your* search, was a typical "crisis" situation. The three main steps (Facts, Feelings, Wants) allow us to work through the business at hand in a methodical fashion. It creates focus in our own consciousness. Quite often, growth does begin with a crisis situation. The crisis is either forced on you by external circumstances, or *you must artificially induce a crisis* to make the process real and shake yourself from apathy. If you allow yourself to be overcome with apathy, then all exercises to help you will be wasted.

Level IV is the next band of exploration. Once Level III is defined, what are your wishes and wants beyond that? You can start taking bolder steps now! For example, our friend has rightly reassured himself he has skills that another company could use; even after the destructive anguish of his self-doubt. If he developed some other skills, either by planned training or personal re-direction, could he become a salesman of plastic mouldings or even start his own firm, specialising in the most sophisticated and profitable components?

You will never have the nerve to contemplate Level IV if you decide you are destined to stay at Level II or III. So many people consciously *choose* to agonise over their bad fortunes and the mortgage that threatens them at every turn! Worrying guarantees a muddled head, and saps vital energy away to a bottomless pit. That is why you must lead yourself through the stages, each stage leading to a higher level of clear perspectives and possibilities.

Look back on your life for a moment. How many of the worries, fears and terrors that you anguished over came to pass? Was your house re-possessed when the mortgage rate went up? Did the big ends fail on your old car as you expected them to? Did your teenage daughter run off with a cult after all, fulfilling your greatest fears about her wild curiosity? Was that abdominal pain what you thought it might be at first? Worry pens us in, overwhelms us, makes us weak, rattles our knee-joints. It causes butterflies in the stomach and snakes in the intestines. In any worrying situation, assess what the *worst possible outcome could be.* Assume that the worst would happen. Would it necessarily ruin you? Could you see ways to deal with it, bad as it could be? You will notice that honesty and resignation to the situation generates solutions, not problems. And worrying is an extra burden you can dispense with altogether. In deciding what you may want from life, dispense with worry. Say

"Enough!" Worry will only set boundaries and conditions on your skill to navigate through the fog.

There is today, and there is tomorrow. A state of equilibrium which makes sense of both *can be achieved* in your life. What is best for you will suggest itself, by intuition more than reason. Whether it's running your own company or having a lifetime's supply of toilet rolls. Use your focused mind to flesh out the things you want. *Beware of the unfocused, chattering mind of I want I want I want.* Level IV will then be lots of fun for you. That's where you set some goals for yourself; later I'll explain how you're going to see them come true. Chapter 5 has been a warm-up session to make you think about yourself in a logical way. It may have failed to clarify exactly what you should be doing with your life; don't expect conclusive insights this early. But first, some insights and warnings about the ways we become overwhelmed by external events, and the hands of fate.

Six   Upwaves, Downwaves

Our individual, unique perception of events and experiences can be a measure of our own insecurity. Every one of us sees this world differently. We see other people differently. How do you perceive yourself? To some, the world is a living hell, and they don't have to be living in Beirut. Others in similar circumstances are floating along on a joyful cloud, seeing wonder and beauty everywhere. Which person is more in touch with reality? We are routinely inundated with information on the state of the world. It is difficult to deny that it affects us. The external world is there alright, but must we be intimidated by it?

Start watching the television news regularly every evening. Try to concentrate on the issues and the basic communication of facts. What proportion of the news is essentially *bad* news? Make a judgement after five news programmes at least. Keep a pad and pencil by your TV chair. You will find that you are learning about confrontation somewhere: wars, terrorism, a murder or an accident, a pollution story, a sex scandal, a long-winded intrigue involving people in high places, rising inflation, the closure of another big plant, someone suing someone else, people complaining about living conditions and injustice, politicians snarling at their adversaries. How often do you learn of a really pleasant event happening somewhere in the world, especially things which affect the lives of ordinary people? Try this exercise; you might be surprised how negatively our world is described to us.

Dramatists aim for confrontation and conflict as a matter of course. They develop all sorts of complications to give the play substance, and often just to spin it out. When the complications get to the overload stage, we must have a crisis. A catastrophe is the smart twist to the story which brings us down again, where our heroes meet their deserved success and the tyrants get chased. A nice conclusion winds up the evening.

Are we witnessing a prepared form of drama on the news each night? Do magazine articles build up dramatic effect? Are newspapers sensational, or are they not? Is there an obsessive motivation towards selling in most forms of the media? Salesmanship is a way of life. Who will watch or read news about some family in Wiltshire that is attending the graduation of their adopted son, a boy who survived the boat exodus from Vietnam? Or interviews with the colourful characters who tackle inner city transformation using their hands, not their mouths? It makes unspectacular news.

All news affects you. *Try ignoring all sources of news or media discussion for two weeks,* and consciously move away from others who are debating the current tragedies, horrors, or intrigues. Sometimes we invite criticism from the "information die-hards" should we choose to tune out from society's "troubles". That is a selfish act! Whatever the issues, your indifference may bring you contempt. News of urban violence depresses you: you tune out. Then you experience conflict from someone criticising your lack of compassion! People keep themselves informed of the world's problems as a *partial purpose to life.* We are urged to take heed and believe that the experts are always right, because they have more *data* than us. The doom-peddlers pass the gloomy consensus down to us, like a gift. A shift of guilt occurs. Together, we create a dubious new morality based on miserable people, all wrapped up in current affairs!

Some say we become what we eat. That may not be as accurate as what we become through stuffing ourselves with information, that we did not create ourselves. We can refuse food we can't abide, or our stomachs will reject it for us. But how do we handle the banquet of information pressed on us daily? We seek out information like vital sustenance, craving it and thriving on it. Quiet everyone, the news is on, we must partake.

The individual person is seen by many these days purely as an economic unit. We are described in terms of interest rates, housing costs, salary levels, cost-of-living index, inflation, and credit risk (to name a few). The life of the world and all who tread on it is fuelled by political factors, debt, recessions, booms, crises, competition, technology changes, and good old fate. As individuals, we struggle with our basic survival, pay insurance on all we gather, and prepare for old age. As we progress, the system tells us our self-worth is largely specified by and through money. A bad day in the financial

City of London affects Wall Street in a matter of hours. The consequences are explained by the investment consultants on the six o'clock news. Interest rates are moving again. Mortgage payments might change next month. The reduced money supply may mean restricted borrowing and company layoffs. We are all caught up in the big global cycles. Some are winning, some losing. Who can we believe any more? Is it worth buying a house, or better to rent? Do shares make sense for someone approaching retirement? What will gold do next year? Can I trust the advice of fee-hungry experts on investing my money, whether it's now in tin mines or wrapped in a sock? What exactly controls the whole thing, and where do I fit into that? Fear and confusion are inevitable. Too many negative facts, then comes the surrender of the will, the fear to act at all. Confidence disappears long before this. We believe that *other people are understanding the system: that's why they're successful.* They must have inside information.

"My house is losing value, while others are retiring at fifty on their profits. My small business went bust in a year. That man up the street is employing four more people this week. It's this damned world recession. When's it going to end? Every time I have a good idea, there's a world recession! They say things are getting better after the last trade figures. Order books filling up, new opportunities everywhere. Why can't I find a job? Everyone's lying. The news is full of useless facts that can't help me."

Finding someone or something to blame is great fun. You have so many choices. Several bricks have gone through television screens for this very reason! We like to blame the system, society, the banks, big business, politicians and God. Blaming God is especially popular, when the going is really tough. We can imagine God heaping on the problems, testing us, warning us, punishing us. It's a nice theory, but quite wrong. God neither imposes the problem, nor solves it. But He does *care* about our many predicaments, crises, episodes of anguish and pain. Knowing that gives us strength to cope. We would all like a perfect world, perfect lives, no downwaves, ever. Since we live in a real world, we look for guilty parties. Family members are also popular as targets for blame.

My parents are to blame for the way I've turned out. My father lived in his own world of keeping other people's books and pretending he was a Chartered Accountant. His idea of excitement was a freemason's meeting once in a blue moon. Mother was always in the house, the garden, or in shops. I can't think of where else she spent any significant time, apart from visiting an elderly friend on Thursday afternoons.

They gave me what could be expected, I suppose. We got along, in a fashion. Other than asking if I had homework or dirty washing from football, my education was a mystery to them. Dad would ask when my next exams were, then forget to ask how I had done. Really, we hardly knew each other.

When I left home, I went a bit wild. It was the feeling of freedom. My first year at university was great, but I failed all but one subject. The idea of repeating everything was absurd; I dropped out and went to work as a dishwasher in a Spanish hotel. From then on, I had jobs here, jobs there. I can't say I've been in any place for more than a year. Recently I had a serious accident coming home from a party with a car I borrowed. I wasn't hurt badly, but the other chap was. The whole thing's like a punishment.

I get these notions about starting again, but that's impossible with my background. If only I had parents with some contacts, instead of a dreary pair of lower middle-class bores. They didn't encourage me much, nor did they help me to start off right in the first place. How could they? They were lost in a deeper rut than me, and I hate them for it.

This young man is very effective in passing the blame to others. He does it with great energy and enthusiasm. In a sense, he is probably right. A father estranged from his son, by reason of his simple lifestyle. A mother who was "just a housewife". What problems did the father have? Was he ashamed of his status, pretending he was a real accountant? Did the freemasons' meetings give him a sense of belonging or identity, that his son never gave to him? And what exactly were his mother's motives in visiting an elderly person? Perhaps she was having a superb time sharing funny stories with a lively old soul, whereas she had to endure two uncaring males at home. Parents are humans too. They are just as likely to be confused or in a mess with *their lives*. At least, they don't have access to all the answers just because they are parents.

His parents were failures in his eyes, and have no means of helping him now. In a material or practical sense, that might be so. However, he lived his own life in the big wide world and it turned out to be a failure. Why did he waste his chance at university? Blame it on the parents for misunderstanding his genius! Why did he drift from one hole to another? Blame them forever! Now, a car-crash in a borrowed car. He is punishing himself, and that is great fun too! He is very effective at bashing *himself* on the head with a hammer. Maybe he could get a job as a stonemason or a sculptor! If he cannot get help from his parents, then he is *giving up*. It's all their fault that life is unfair. If he keeps pounding away with his hammer, he will soon be able to sign over his life to counsellors and psychologists. They might have the answers.

This person is caught in a downwave of self-imposed circumstances. Inflation is not the immediate problem, nor the unemployment statistics. While waiting for the next upwave, he amuses himself by blaming his parents for all his misfortunes. This could go on indefinitely. He says that he gets notions about starting again. But he feels that his background defeats this right away. Laziness to act is his central problem: not his background. The secret is for him to forget his attachments to the past. He can see that his parents cannot help. Correct. But why not just love them, as confused and unspectacular parents, and stop looking for answers in them that they don't have?

Many difficult and unfair situations do have blame components in them. Wicked people causing unpleasant or damaging circumstances is one example. If they had acted in a different and more compassionate way, miseries could be avoided. Unfortunately, they are *free to act as they will,* and through lack of judgement, or sheer callousness, hurtful events are born. Fingers can be pointed, but *how long* can you hold your arm up in anger? Instead of finding others to blame, move on swiftly to the immediate problem: *you.* Stop seeing yourself as persecuted, betrayed, unlucky, unjustly wronged, a failure; someone who will never achieve anything worthwhile because of others, or the past.

What you do have control over, is your freedom. But how on earth could you have freedom in a world so structured and controlled? How can it be, when the system is so tightly strung that a one-percent rise in interest rates destroys thousands of small businesses? Whether you see it as responsible or not, *you have the freedom to opt out.* You can choose to *think* freely and effectively, with all the noise and turbulence of the system tuned out.

Once you can grasp the reality of being in the world, but not necessarily compelled by it, you can make some progress. There is no need to drop right out of society and go to the nearest commune just to think. Some have tried living in monasteries or other inspirational centres. If that is what you must do, feel free. However, most people will opt to sort themselves out while paying the mortgage and the milkman.

You need to determine where you are, relative to the noise out there. Your illusions or your theories about the world have to be put into hibernation for a while. No need to laugh at tragedy when you hear of it, nor ignore the reminders on your outstanding electric bill. Just realise that you must rise above the fuss and the facts out there. There are certainly downwaves. (How many recessionary cycles have we had, with unemployment and misery everywhere?). Upwaves and downwaves. (Look at the Stock Market surges in 1986 and the crashes in 1987). You are neither a subject of nor a pawn in the game played by the Big Boys. Unless you believe you are.

We tend to follow the crowd because it is easy. Shaking off cosy illusions is painful; standing apart, lonely. We have collective beliefs, never our own. When fate deals us a cruel blow, we feel it is not due to the normal processes of life and reality, but a personal kick in the shins from the system. When things go well, we think we have been clever and have done all the right things. It is fun to prove our life-theories to ourselves. After all, we like to believe they give life meaning.

Work and career building is a good source of enlightenment in fate. Whatever the company is doing, it affects us. Employment gives us a personal stake in the upwave/downwave game. We want our firm to do well, because that gives us more security and a chance of career growth. By grooming ourselves in what we do, we hope to enjoy constantly increasing expectations, a better fate. Our ideas of work, wages and effort are loosely related to the larger world picture of achieving "progress". That progress is interpreted as our personal upwave, should we be on the winning end. If you are prospering in the Information Technology sector, recession is a relative term for you. A dairy farmer facing bank foreclosures and ruin can only see himself on a downwave and he curses the Government, the banks, the EEC and maybe even his parents!

Work as a human pastime has achieved a very high profile in our perception of the world. At election time, people interviewed in the street always blame the Government for not doing anything about unemployment. In areas of high employment, they still complain. Are our lives nothing without work? For many people, work is the point of focus in contemplating upwaves and downwaves. Work makes their lives; lack of it destroys them. A job can be a substitute for the meaning of life to many people; it is larger than life. Work commands us. Career building is a demonstration of self-worth and ego for many. Men are particularly bound up in the ladders of status, competition and outward success. The demands are infinite on the willing. Without conscious choices, men become mere machines to sustain ever-increasing family lifestyles. Women in the career game are no less misled. Employment is not ultimate truth, it is simply hiring your time out for a price. Work gives us something to build illusions on. We like to think it protects us from tragedies; well, some of the time.

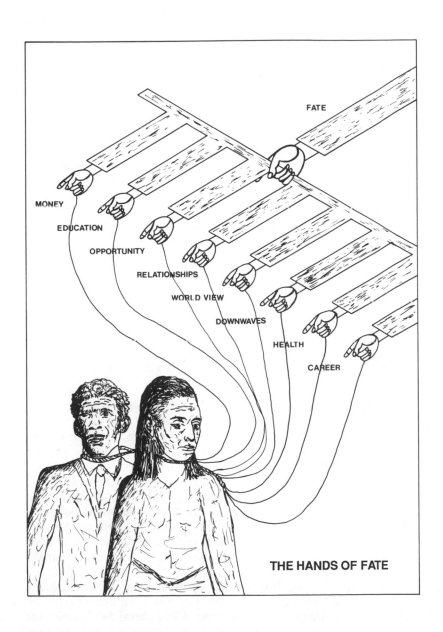

THE HANDS OF FATE

I was sketching something at my desk, unaware of the time, but conscious that the coffee had not passed. I visualised my cheese sandwich wrapped in cling-film; that would get the morning under way.

A fluorescent light nearby was starting to flicker. The daily coffee group was late. It was quiet in the office today. I wandered over to see what Tessa might be sticking on her paste-up boards. The marking pens, cutting knives and bottles of white paint lay on her table.

The group stood behind a row of cabinets, talking quietly. We studied each other's faces.

"Well, that's the drawing office wiped out", one said.

Eight people, I considered. Tessa had often given me recipes to try. One chap had solved my car problems. Another had confided to me his desolation after divorce. The group was wiped out, redundant, unwanted.

As the day wore on, the number doubled. People were receiving phone calls like breaths from the Grim Reaper. The phone beside me rang. This is it, I thought. Am I ready to take this thing?

"Is Mike there?"

"No, but I'll find him".

I escaped the day's layoffs. I felt drained, almost hung-over. The terror perhaps, or relief manifesting itself as fatigue. A single selfish thought shocked me: "I'm still in, they didn't sack me, I'm of value here!" There was a fundamental difference between people in this world, I reasoned. Some lose, others don't. Survival of the fittest. I was happy about that. It's human, of course, to feel sorry at the time. My soul was still in the right place. Anyway, I'd never see those people again most likely.

Business returned to normal, and the remaining staff regrouped quickly. A new organisation chart was prepared. Fear was always there, but things looked brighter with less payroll costs. I went home one Friday to fry trout and maybe open a bottle of supermarket wine. I felt good, content. The phone rang while the fish crackled in the pan. It was a simple message, and I understood it easily. You are terminated effective immediately; a letter will be sent to you with the details.

We know the feeling. When the other person loses the dash against fate and is swallowed up, we feel that odd flush of embarrassed relief. Not me! They deserved it maybe, it's their karma, or their wickedness being redressed by God, fair and square. We smugly assume that somehow the world makes sense: it's not all haphazard chaos and chance. Yet when dreaded phone calls or letters *do afflict us,* it's an entirely different world. Out come the torrents of blame, the theories on justice, the world view of bitter cynicism, anger and hurt. Whether it's a lost job or a loved one lost to drug addiction, we cannot build futures on bitterness. Easy to write, to read, you say, but difficult to implement. Nevertheless, if we are to make the best of our lives, the question is not *Why?* but *What now?*

The moment we think we understand the facts, or the theories, cycles, rules or patterns, we are abruptly reminded that all our illusions are more notional than sensible. All of them! We studied the news, the facts, logic and trends. We studied our career path and took courses to prepare for better things. We had watertight personal philosophies of how rewards were allocated, how punishments inflicted. Then fate descends on us out of the blue and burns the trout! Does fate have the final word? Dealing with fate is a process of letting go, *accepting what is;* refusing to cling to facts, theories, illusions, angry battles over justice. But then, we delight in avoiding reality.

It is a true fact that educated, intellectual and well-informed people often fail miserably in entrepreneurial ventures. While they are studying some trend or other, they lose an order to their competitor (who works out of his garden shed and has one O-level, in arithmetic). The experts have little imagination; they are stuffed with facts and theories, and they are generally fearful about every step they take. They dress up their doubts and draw impressive graphs using spreadsheets on their computers.

The true thinker has a humble but open mind. He is honest with himself, and admits he hasn't a clue when faced with information on all fronts. His strength lies in *facing problems squarely, making decisions, and making them quickly.* (Isn't that what everyday life is all about?). Making wrong decisions doesn't trouble him at all. He presses on and enjoys being different, right or wrong. As he experiences the hard realities of his decisions, he grows smart, and learns how to be right more often. The other fellow is exhausting himself, trying to find a database bureau that can predict how the world will be in ten years' time! The perfectionist can talk about the problems for hours, but defers the move towards solutions. He can show you results of various studies. But if he has refused to think apart from the din, he will eventually discover reality and be hurt by it. Not fate: *reality.*

Decision-making in large organisations can sometimes be an interesting study in brilliant procrastination. As the organisations become more complex, and the advent of information technology becomes fully adolescent, the scope is limitless. The speed and dexterity of computer networks give us the means of accessing vast amounts of data, and manipulating it. Corporate decision-making is normally based on some accepted rules of order:

Terms of reference (chairman's ideas, concerns)
Defining the problem or the need for change
Interviews and discussion sessions
Fact analysis and classification
Generation and evaluation of alternatives
Presentation of findings with reasoning

With complex issues involving resources of people, capital, and physical facilities, the process is essentially rational. It is especially relevant for production, marketing and distribution operations. When applied to less tangible problems, the results suffer the consequences of trying to put everything through the same machine.

There are instances where management consultants are brought in to solve the problems, to devise brilliant decisions for management to implement. After months of gathering the facts, looking at them, classifying them, and forming possible solutions from them, the client decides to do nothing. Quietly, the magnificent report documents are sent to the corporate archives!

The core dynamics of a company management team will embody the analytical people, the strictly profit-motivated ones, the structured thinkers, and the traditionalists. Some space might be kept for a few "lost souls", and perhaps one true visionary who dreams half the time. It is wrong to say that any particular faction forms the best decision-making elite.

Each of the members has his or her own world view. They have their perceptions of the news and current information, and their personal relationship to the environment in which they must operate. Their collective effect is similar to that of an individual, only more diverse. They all have a duty to act out a role, whether it is comfortable for them or not. Meanwhile, the external world is changing things, giving them more problems to solve. As a group, they should fare better than individuals dealing with the same set of problems. But even with all the best brains assembled, using the most sophisticated business tools, blunders are still made. By the time they analyse everything, the next upwave or downwave comes along! The moral of the story? Don't feel that you are at a disadvantage, relative to those you think should know so much better!

When we trust facts or computers (even in the hands of experts) to make our decisions for us, we are kidding ourselves. Of course, when a decision goes wrong, we can blame the computer. We might even find a way to blame our parents, or God, or the price of molasses on the commodities market!   Better to spend the time understanding how lost we make ourselves by relying on all those external things. Blaming others, or the system, wastes precious energy. Refusing to distance ourselves from our love of reason will lead us into more of the same: *educated confusion.*

There are no upwaves or downwaves in the world you choose to see. Only you, today, and tomorrow. *Listen to yourself for a change; switch off the experts.* They take up such a lot of your time, and absorb your energy. Once you learn to live beyond their "help", you can watch and read *for contrast, not direction.* The world is not as finite or as fatalistic as you might think, or as you have been told. Don't waste your life waiting for the next upwave. It might arrive too late for you to even see it. Furthermore, living life as a process of good and bad luck, waiting for the winds to reverse, is also likely to be frustrating. One of the basic rules of life, is that fairness may not be possible. Another rule, however, is that we always have the power to act, to make choices, and to do so cheerfully, even when we'd like to scream.

Part III

What are your goals, and how will you achieve them?

"Goals! Dreams you mean! My goals came to nought".

"It all sounds so simple, but life just isn't like that. I *know* ".

"Yes I could be a better person, more prosperous too. But every time I try, the next hurdle knocks me down".

"I tried thinking positive once. People thought I was soft in the head".

"My attitudes might be wrong, but success isn't my destiny, whether I change or not".

"Playing with your mind is weird. It frightens me".

Seven   Setting Goals: Why Not?

The secret of success is constantly to purpose.

Benjamin Disraeli

You might not like the term "goals". Perhaps it's an unfortunate word for you. You might consider another word, such as ambitions, choices, desires, wishes, aspirations, aims, directions, endeavours, purposes. The reason? The word "goals" has unhappily become associated with career-hungry executives and greedy people building their self-centred Utopias. (Real success is not the successful outcome of greed). Choose whatever word suits you, or stick with goals for convenience.

We are not accustomed to stating categorically what we are going to have. As children, it is second nature. "When I'm big, I'm going to have a car, an aeroplane, a big house, and a big farm with thousands of golden hamsters". If we could just harness the power of imagination we had then! As adults, we are more subdued. We don't go around saying we are going to be earning twice as much next year. Rather than appearing complete fools next year, we simply wait and see.

There is an element of excitement attached to knowing what you want, after honestly opening up to yourself. When you have clear ideas of the type of things you want in your life, there will be an air of great expectation in you. That assumes you have disposed of the negative connotations about having goals. If you believe that your gain is another's loss, either you are an austere person by nature, or you don't understand the reason for the gift of life you have in you.

Some false aesthetics have been built up over the years about goals. Various schools of positive thinking and management grooming have driven the practice of setting goals almost to its death. Employers at staff interviews glibly ask about five-year-goals, or next year's targets. Are we caught up in a Wonderland game of croquet, where we lose our heads if we can't score? "Give me one negative thought, and there's no jam for *you* today!"

A complete jargon has arisen over the years, in the business of getting you to better yourself. There has to be a "gameplan". There's always an "action list". A "critical path" to somewhere. Some sort of "performance indicators" or "criteria". A set of "functional parameters" maybe. Impressive words! It is time to begin a new and less esoteric set of terms. How about: I'm lost; I could be in a rut; I need help; I think I can find a way forward? Don't ever be intimidated by the generous theories on "successful thinking" in so many learned books and papers. Just make sure you are comfortable with your own ideas and feelings.

Approach your goal definition with enthusiasm, and do it cheerfully. If you treat it as an exercise in futility, choose to remain where you are. You are responsible for what you do, so do it well. And do it on your own. Allow your partner or your friends into this programme and you might not hear the vital whispers for the babble. All you need right now is a classical sceptic or a well-meaning comedian to knock your goals, aims, endeavours for six! You are at your weakest point in this entire process right now. Sharpen those pencils again. Thinking is no good. Thinking *and* writing might get you there.

We discovered there were two distinct types of goal: material and personal. You prepared inventories of how these stand with you at the present time. Then you gave some thought to possible "wants" in your life. Those wants were extensions of your present reality and circumstances. The chart with the six sectors focused on *you* at the centre, at a specific point in time. To attempt Level IV, take a leap across the boundary, and demonstrate that you have learned something about being an Open Person.

You may have scratched your head getting to Level III. You feel satisfied that your present situation can improve if you just apply yourself a bit. So far, you've relied on *logic and the reasoning mind,* suitably focused on the situation you are in, and possibly tired of. You have used your imagination to come up with several possibilities, rather than more proof to call yourself a failure. The process automatically comes up with "wants".

The question now is whether or not you will continue into Level IV with only a list of basic wants. I want a better job. I want more money. I want new friends. I want to control my behaviour. In your heart of hearts, do you believe that Level III is going to be sufficient for you? It was suggested that the Kingston fellow consider a business of his own. He seems to know his stuff, but the company doesn't realise his ambition. Will that be *his* leap to Level IV in the Career sector? Or deep down, does he *really want* to be a weaver of fine cloths in a Welsh cottage, doing Bed & Breakfast in the summer? You have reached the point of truth: a boundary of personal subtleties tied to *real change*.

The procedures used in reaching Level III led you to possibilities which might become goals. If you did nothing to flesh out possibilities, or wants, then you might flounder about indefinitely.The material and personal aspects are interrelated, whatever you decide to carry into Level IV. On crossing the boundary, then, remain flexible and open. If starting a business is the thing for you, then so be it. Think of the personal qualities you'll need for that business.

Let your thoughts run free, but stay focused. Don't let the restraining influence of Level III take the fun out of Level IV. You might say the wants of Level III are attainable, with a little effort and control. They are baby goals, based on what you know best. They are active decisions based on available facts and feelings. Remember what was said about dreamers, that they were the ones to watch? Well, feel free to dream a bit. Have fun!

PERSONAL GOALS

These come first. The aim isn't to become a bad-mouthed, un-forgiving, stressful, immature and opinionated millionaire! If your personal goals are in order, you will find that the material ones will be less difficult to achieve, *and to enjoy.*

Return to Chapter 4 and consider both the questions and the answers you gave in the Personal Review. You will re-discover some latent ideas if you look. In particular, check these:

Personal Attributes

Self-confidence is a must. Are you in agreement? Persistence took you this far. Are you still in? People really do matter. Are you having problems there? Does change give you nightmares or excitement?

Interpersonal Maturity

Do you agree that others might know more than you? Insecurities are like shadows. Can you name yours? Is the external world still getting to you? Have you really tried to be an Open Person?

Skills

You *must* have some skills, or you're being hard on yourself. Are your skills "you" or have they just happened by default? Could present skills lead on to other things, given some imagination?

Special Skills

Do you consider these secondary or important? Are you embarrassed by these private skills? Could you sell or apply these skills in any way?

Satisfying Returns

Have you noticed any strong patterns here? Is money the only factor in any of these activities? Have you *felt the sheer pleasure in doing them?* Were they things that you feel you must continue?

Direction

Are you adding up to anything other than money? Have you any faith in anything, including yourself? Are you reading all this without belief? Has apathy got a firm hold of you?

Personal goals are easy to define, but difficult to implement. Growth is demanding and frustrating: your goal might be to have a cheerful disposition, but gloomy circumstances ridicule your efforts. We often consciously avoid the goals which we know will give us the most problems and pain (but they are essential to our progress). You might fiercely criticise people who blatantly pick their noses at a business meeting or the dinner table. Then, in private, you have a session with your own nose that lasts for hours! This is not serious goal material, but use the analogy! If you think that by writing goals you will solve problems, think again. You must *want the goals to happen, and you must change your behaviour as far as that demands.* So don't have a goal on paper that you set out to circumvent and defy!

The chart you completed had "Personal" and "Relationships" among the sectors. Study what you developed in Level II under these headings. Are you aware of the weaknesses you have in these areas, and some ideas of what you want to change? Allow yourself a warmup session to work through these ideas (on paper). Once you have the picture reasonably steady, draft up some goals. Since the goals are yours, and yours alone, write them in your own style and choice of language. This is important. Copying set pieces from another's list has no personal connection with you, even if the nature of the goal is identical.

To give you a structure to work towards, examples of personal goals follow. Notice the sequence of preparing the background, before drafting the goal. Although the result is merely a page of words, make sure you think through your motivation in building each goal. Write your goal in the present tense, as though it is already true. And feel the power of your own words. If you are a shy person, and feel that this holds you back in many things, "Confidence" is an obvious choice. As you explore the reasons why you want to be more confident, face up to the very things that cause you embarrassment (awkward speech, hand waving, agitation). Visualise what you might look like if you controlled your breathing, sat erect, looked the person in the eye without blushing, and so on. That is what is meant by *feeling the power of your own words.* When your goal rings a certain bell within you, it must be overdue. If a goal feels right, if it raises your interest and excitement, it's right for you.

LIST OF PERSONAL GOALS: FULL FORM

HONESTY

Background

I find myself distorting the truth quite often in the average day. Sometimes it gets out of hand. I fabricate stories which are so believable, people trust my stories explicitly. My imagination is vivid, so I find it easy to string people along. I'm a salesman of business forms and stationery. The trouble is, my memory is getting worse as I get older. I get myself into shocking jams where a story comes back to trip me up. Worse than all of this: I often lose track of the truth altogether. I actually think things happened, and they didn't. What started as a habit is making me a complete and unconditional liar.

If I keep going on like this, I'll lose my mind. I feel guilty about lying to people, whether I'm conscious of it or not. Sooner or later, I'll make a fatal blunder and lose a big order, or someone will pass the word I'm a lying toad. I'll lose my job. My wife tolerates it and laughs at my peculiarity. I don't see the funny side any more. I'm scared and want to stop this nonsense.

Goal

I am honest whenever I speak to people. If I am uncertain of the truth at that instant, I stop talking and prevent myself from chattering on with no control.

Before going out on a day's calls, I write out a brief for each firm I visit. The brief states exactly what I am going for, how I will handle the meeting, and what things are necessary in the discussion.

I have a line of banter which has nothing to do with work, and used only for entertaining clients and winning them round. It is sincere and repeatable. I write things down if I must.

PATIENCE

Background

When a report has to go out at work, I wind up like an alarm clock. I always get my side of things done, even if I work late all week. It's when it reaches the publication and binding stage I get impatient. I have to rely on so many people to get it out. When my back is turned, they're off to brew up tea or have a smoke. I check the time every ten minutes or so; when I forget, I panic because a whole half-hour has disappeared. Just watching the others work at their pathetic pace makes me boil. Often, I tell them to clear out and I do the damned thing myself. Of course, that's no joy either.

Other people are going to give me a heart attack, I know it. Why should they have the satisfaction? I lose sleep while the process is under way. I dream of punching holes in stacks of paper streaming out of the photocopier. My health will suffer. Besides, I find I can't get along with the staff after these panic episodes. I want to be friendly towards them, but I get snubbed. Even the boss sees that I'm staying in my office all the time, avoiding contact.

Goal

I plan the report operation long before the crunch. I study the steps involved and see where the bottlenecks are.

I invite all the print-room and word-processing people to a meeting. I'm the chairperson, but they do the talking. We work out a system. Before each report is at the final stages, we have a strategy meeting for an hour, to agree on what we're all doing. I tell myself the time is worth it, and relax in the knowledge that we are a team in control. The result of this: I'm a patient person.

SELF-RESPECT

Background

I lost my job six months ago. I've tried all the usual ways: I'm sure they say "Well, if he was any good, he'd have a job by now". I can see it in their faces, if I actually get to an interview. I find myself walking about the town to pass the time. All the things you think you'll do if you didn't have to work, well, I don't do them. I sit in the library with other misfits, killing time. Sometimes I look at the Yellow Pages, but that's a waste. I think my skills are out of date and I'm too fed up to go on any courses, free or not. When I go swimming or to the cinema in working hours, their eyes rub it in you're a loser. I only shave every other day now. I stopped seeing friends in the evenings. My shoes never saw polish in weeks. When I go to the photocopy shop to get CV's done, I feel it more than ever; the girl knows what I'm doing. I can't hide the fact I'm a failure.

When I get an interview, my shoes are polished, but I'm a bit dejected. It probably shows. Friends have abandoned me because all I talk about is not having a job, and putting myself down. I feel like an outcast, no longer a member of society. A tramp that sleeps on the river-bank on warm afternoons. I know I'm on some sort of downward spiral. I doze off in a chair. I watch TV without concentrating at all. I sleep in regularly. I eat when I feel like it. I can see myself slipping all right.

Goal

Every day, I achieve *something* to get myself up and running again; even if it's a small thing. Each day, I review what I did to improve my self-respect, *however small*.

I actually forget I'm unemployed, and tell myself that my daily "work" is experiencing life as normal, but I don't have to physically go to work. I treat myself as equal to any person with a job; I am not inferior in any way. I actually feel good, having re-established my value as a person.

WILLPOWER

Background

I've tried working on a plan for my life and career before. It didn't get off the ground. I think that's when my son had measles or something. I went on a public speaking course once. That inspired me to be a part-time lecturer at the local Technical College. I filled in the forms, but pulled out before the interview. It meant driving five miles in winter, with an ageing car. My husband said I should do an Open University course to better myself. I did enrol for one in psychology. I was interested, but I couldn't see myself getting a degree. So I stopped doing the assignments and lost my fee.

I really want to do something more than work in someone else's camera shop. I like photography, but my mind's full of other ideas too. Looking back, I can see a sorry trail of pipe-dreams and false starts. And what a waste of time and money too! I'm the type of person who comes home with twelve library books, determined to find an interest. Then I take them back in a week, unopened. I don't want to be like this, but it just seems to happen.

Goal

I have found an interest that endures the test of time. From the start, I have stuck to it, even when I must deal with other problems and distractions. I keep a journal, and note down every day what I did to bring my special interest forward.

My husband supports me by discussing what my interest is about. He asks specific questions to see if I'm progressing!

When I see results on this project, I will select another interest and make sure it reaches completion. I welcome this habit of imposed self-discipline.

SINCERITY

Background
The other girls at the bank are extremely evasive when it comes to talking about themselves. I find myself doing it too now. We have conversations about work, or buses being late, but we are insincere about our real feelings. There is tension when you innocently ask someone if they'll stick this branch, or try for a posting. It extends to where we spend our evenings. Some pretend they went to some classy restaurant, just to seem flash or prove some vague point. It's a game of half-truths, withholding information, and deflecting questions. It never used to be like this. I find I'm taking my office insincerity outside work, and being misleading with good friends. I even sidestep my mother about relationships, when really there's nothing to hide, and I'd desperately like to talk. It's a work habit that drives my whole attitude.

I notice that my behaviour is making friends suspicious of me, because I'm giving them less than the whole truth! We end up with shallow communication. Who wants to discuss the weather, or the price of tights, instead of real heart-to-hearts with people you trust? I used to enjoy being open with people; it made me feel good. I feel more like myself anyway when I'm being sincere. It's stressful keeping that restraint up all the time. I know the world isn't as honest as it could be, but I'm certain I'm losing present and potential friends over this.

Goal
I am sincere to all people, whatever way they behave with me. I acknowledge that I will be vulnerable, but if I'm open and honest, I know it'll make them think about their position.

I trust people from the start and show that trust. I do understand that people want to be sincere, and I will create an environment for that to happen. My sincerity will help others.

DECISIVENESS

Background

I was glad to get the position of Social Work Director. The second woman to hold a job at that level in this city! After the early excitement was over, I got down to the serious business of doing the job. We had presentations from education and charity people. I would sum up and establish priorities. The department heads (all men) would go away and do their own thing. I suppose I went sour on this rejection of my position. To get things done, as I saw necessary, I enlisted support from female supervisors. I found myself ignoring the department heads. We were two camps, and the race was on to beat the men! There were instances of open hostility between the power centres. Then came the budget meetings, which neither group could dominate. Now I'm on the carpet for allowing all this to happen. I thought I did the best thing at the time.

I'm another woman trying to prove herself in a man's world. I am perfectly qualified and capable. The very job I felt was worth doing, I've bungled. I really must get a grip on this, or that coveted job is out the window. Besides, the community is suffering the effects of the war in here. That makes me feel bad.

Goal

I have drafted a plan and called a successful meeting of all department heads, and my Governing Board.

I focus on my level of decisiveness, and I consider events daily to monitor progress of agreed directives. When a member of staff does not agree with a decision, I discuss this privately with him or her. I seek a new consensus if necessary, but my decision is final.

I concentrate on making decisions quickly and with maturity. I act alone, and I accept responsibility for my decisions.

VISION

Background

I know I'll never get rich working for a living. Even if I do overtime for the rest of my life. What I need are ideas to start up on my own. How do some people latch on to a brilliant idea, then make a fortune from it? Sometimes their idea is ridiculous, or so simple I could have dreamt it up. To think I could have done the same as them! In my odd creative moments, I try to come up with schemes to start the ball rolling. I may come up with an idea, but it's never good enough to follow up. I probably don't have the foresight to go further. I know what I have, but what if I were to risk it on some foolish scheme, then fall flat on my face?

There's no doubt, I'm right about working for an employer. I become truly *enthusiastic* away from work, when I search for something new or interesting. I'm probably looking in the wrong places for ideas, though. Being an employee isn't going to satisfy me in the long term. I did try a part-time business a few years ago, and that went well enough. So the main problem lies with finding the right idea to get me off the ground. A sixth sense or something.

Goal

I keep my mind open to all stimuli that come along, with the intent of gathering raw ideas in any area of interest.

I keep an "Ideas File" in which I collect ideas, notes, sketches or cuttings to help me with my goal.

I read magazines in all disciplines to help trigger off ideas I have inside me. I allow my mind to wander sometimes; day-dreaming with a purpose, to generate ideas. At all times, I separate myself from rigid thought patterns and try to see what others miss, in all things and experiences.

Are you getting the general idea of how to develop goals from raw data, loosely contained in your "wants"? It is important to work through the reasoning behind each goal you set. Otherwise, you are being a child: I want I want I want. All the example goals are rooted in a practical environment. Your roots might have nothing to do with work frustrations or surviving a setback. A personal goal might be related to the way you treat your partner. It might be deep-seated resentment that you want to stop, before it devours you. The goal process is very flexible, so use it *for your specific needs*. Be imaginative and resourceful. Design your own goals around the format given. Bring out the facts and the rationale, using your energetic, but focused mind. They don't have to be pretentious or self-analytical; just appropriate to you.

Notice that each goal does not dwell on the problems you are trying to overcome. Don't needlessly remind yourself that you are below the mark in a goal. For example, you might be a selfish, inconsiderate oaf. In your goal, don't write: "I will try to stop being a selfish, inconsiderate oaf". Rather, write : "I am a giving, considerate person, full of generosity and respect for others". And never say "I'm going to...." Say "I am....!" You are *invoking the self-suggestive apparatus here. Tell yourself you are great, and you will be great.* Whether it's curing a stammer or having a winning way with kings. *The possibilities are endless.*

This book cannot give you a catalogue of personal goals to thumb through, nor the convenience of picking some off-the-shelf. That is making life too easy for you. Besides, your goals are for you alone. You need them: you develop them, and define them. Don't overlook the fact that you will be applying them and improving your lot with them!

Generally speaking, you have more chance of achieving your personal goals than ambitious material ones. That is because they are so close to you, and you understand the need more clearly. However, they are perhaps the more tiring, because you are bringing intimate changes into your life. Most personal goals demand changes in your behaviour, and the way you approach the day's events. Each experience contacts you in a new way when you have set yourself the goal to handle it differently. Allow yourself to change. You will get nowhere if you resist change in this life.

MATERIAL GOALS

The scope is open. You can be as timid or as flamboyant as you wish. I would counsel you to err on the wild side. Too much restraint will make you limit possibilities that really should be within your grasp. Your background or your personal hang-ups have nothing to do with the type of material goals you might want to set. If you have a problem with self-confidence, why should that stop you from owning a harpsichord or a racehorse?

Be reasonable though. Everyone is not going to have a Lear Jet, and a Daimler to meet them as they step ashore from their luxury yacht. But if you honestly believe that is where you want to be, *then that is your goal.* Why deny it? It is of no consequence whatsoever that you cannot buy these items right now. Who said anything about *now?*

As you grow into the pattern of commanding success for your life, *the possibilities will present themselves to you.* As an Open Person, with a clear idea of where you are going, you will know the moment an opportunity arrives.

So, choose your material goals with ambition *appropriate to your real desires.* It is foolish to choose a Jaguar XJS with pink seats, just because your last boyfriend got his one repossessed in his downfall! Similarly, don't expect wealth to solve all your problems. Rich people, more than any other group, have a tendency to commit suicide. That doesn't mean that all rich people are statistically unhappy. It just implies that they can be particularly fragile people when the merry-go-round spins too fast. Wealth has a peculiar power to distort reality, introducing excesses and imbalances. Hence the necessary order of personal goals first, material goals second.

You should review your inventory of material things and assets. Know where you stand. You have qualified your Level III "wants". Are you wanting more than you have identified in Level III? Are you restricting your possibilities? Be adventurous! Reach beyond Level III. You may have some ideas bubbling over the boundary already. Stay open and stretch yourself, setting fear and restraint aside. Since the field is so large, it might help to list all the things that catch your eye, then eliminate the absurd and the inappropriate. Pretend that you have won a million on the football pools. How would you spend the money? Go on, draw up a list. In the spirit of make-believe, it seems easier to define material goals, doesn't it? You can prune this list down with a little reason and focus.

LIST OF MATERIAL GOALS: FULL FORM

HOUSE

Background

We live in a terraced house; the walls are so thin I can hear the neighbours sneezing. Most weekends, there's a party somewhere. Every time a door slams, I think there's someone in our place. There's a tiny garden. We can seldom get our car parked near our own door. When the neighbours are all out, I feel like a different person. Maybe my nerves are bothering me, but I don't like this house any more. I stay out a lot when Dave's at work, just to get away from the noise and atmosphere of the place. We haven't bought any more things for the house, because it doesn't seem worth it. We both feel the same way, although I'm probably more upset. What we would like is a good move, to somewhere nice.

This house is causing me stress problems (I have seen the doctor and I had a mild sedative for a while). My husband cannot concentrate on anything creative or do work at home, because of the distractions. We have talked to the neighbours, but the results have never been worth the conflict. The kids would play up, or a row would erupt. We don't enjoy living here any more. We can never relax. Friends notice that we are tense about noise and the feeling of being trapped.

Goal

We own a beautiful house within 40 minutes driving time of Dave's work. It is a three-bedroomed bungalow, set back from the road, and at least 30 yards from the nearest house. It has two bathrooms and a garage/workshop.

The neighbours nearby are people like ourselves who love peace around them. They are friendly and helpful to us.

CAR

Background

I have a Ford Fiesta, now four years old. It's good basic transportation, but starting to give problems. I have driven other cars, and always prefer a 1.8 litre engine at least. They are safer on the road, especially for quick overtaking and getting out of trouble in a hurry. I like driving, but my little Fiesta doesn't give me the feeling of driving a driver's car. As a young woman, I notice that car salesmen always offer you a car like the Fiesta or a Volkswagen Polo! I think I have more adventure to me than that!

My car is reaching the point of trade-in. I am not satisfied with having just a set of wheels to get around on. I am very much an independent thinker, and like to choose what I want for myself. I am a car enthusiast, I suppose, and I love the feeling of a luxury car under my control. The difference between a set of wheels and a thoroughbred car, is like comparing a lump of cheese with dinner at the Ritz!

Goal

I own a Saab 9000i Turbo 16, with all the options I like to see in a quality car. It is white, with dark grey seats. There is a quadraphonic speaker system, with AM/FM cassette and graphic equaliser. It has all-electric power windows, central locking system and an anti-theft alarm. The windows are tinted the same density as the sunroof.

MY OWN BUSINESS

Background

I fix photocopying machines, and I'm on call 7 days a week. I know I'm good at my job, and I've recently finished a home-study course in computer printer maintenance. I've just realised that I could do the same work and have my own business. I'm certain I could make the same money, possibly a lot more, and I'd be my own boss. My wife and kids think it's a great idea. A friend of mine is in the same boat. He repairs computers, so we have a super combination. I've never tried a business before, and I must admit, the idea makes me very anxious.

I have the background skills and enthusiasm to try this. My friend as a partner makes a lot of sense. Together, we could service most of the equipment in offices around town. I know it would be robbing my present firm, but they seem to be more interested in installations than maintenance. I couldn't care less about new installations; what I enjoy is fixing them, and getting them back in service. My family is behind me, so there's no problem there.

Goal

I have a business partnership with my friend. Together, we capture at least 50% of the office equipment repair and servicing work in this town.

We keep spares and equipment in my garage and I've built a car-port for the car. I have taken delivery of a van to make the collection operation more efficient.

I have a rule, that providing the work gets done, both partners enjoy two days off a week to share with family.

WORLD TRAVEL

Background

I am fifty-four years old and have been no further than France and Holland. My hobby is reading travel books and magazines. If there are travel films on in our community centre, I'm always there. For holidays, my wife and I visit relatives. We're not youngsters any more; some of our friends are having heart trouble, or other ailments. I'm quite aware that death is standing behind me, always willing to cart me off! We don't ask much, the pair of us, but we recently discussed the idea of doing things *now*. And travel is the one thing that occupies my dreams most of the time.

We are both in our fifties but really quite fit, with no serious problems. I'll be retiring at sixty (I'm a civil servant), so that's not far away. Then what will I do? I may not be fit enough to go further than Bridlington! I was always a procrastinator about doing what I'd really like to do, but now I feel that *time is running out*. My best pal had a mild heart attack three months ago, and that brought it home. We're not exactly well-off, and not the type to go gallivanting about. But we feel it would be something to remember as we get older.

Goal

I have selected the countries of the world we want to visit, and a route to take them all in. I have chosen a variety of transport, rather than just flights, to get a feel for each place.

I have discussed our plans with my manager and taken steps to arrange a 3 month leave of absence. My wife and I have selected a travel agent and started the bookings.

LEARNING TO FLY/MY OWN AIRCRAFT

Background

My younger brother was in the Combined Cadet Force at school, and did a lot of flying about in gliders and Chipmunks. He had a great time. Being a girl, I had to concentrate on being in the badminton team, and learning how to be beautiful. I really envied my brother, but of course never admitted it. I used to secretly don his flying overalls and helmet, before he went out to the nearby RAF base. When we went on holiday one year, he rented a glider and took my dad up. But I had to stay with mum and hold her hand! Every time I see small planes, I go berserk. I'm more enthusiastic than my brother ever was. So I went out to the local airfield and took their half-price lesson in a Cessna! I haven't calmed down since.

I know my eyes and health are alright. There's nothing in the world I'd rather do, than learn to fly. I'm separated; maybe my wild ambition has something to do with that! Financially, I'll get my fair share, but supporting myself will be a concern. Nevertheless, I feel drawn to flying. I believe it will give me something worthwhile, an achievement which I can use to build a new life around.

Goal

I have a Private Pilot's Licence and Night Rating. My logbook shows my solo time greatly exceeding my dual time, giving me experience towards my Commercial Licence.

I own a Cessna 182 with full panel flight instruments, twin VOR receivers, ADF, transponder and basic Instrument Landing System. It is blue and white, with dark blue seats.

I operate my own Air Taxi and Charter service, employing a commercial pilot. I do aerial photography and motorway patrols for the police.

Heady stuff, isn't it? To just sit down at your desk and specify the number of bathrooms, your van for the business, and the colour of your aircraft's seats! With the sheer audacity of assuming the goals are already achieved, and the keys to your car or Cessna are in your hand right now!

The last thing you want to feel is uncomfortable. You do want those things you have specified, don't you? If not, now is the time to pick the essential goals from the nonsense ones. But if you want that Cessna, leave it on the list: no goal you want badly enough is ever nonsense.

The "Full Form" goals, both Personal and Material, must now be reduced to a pocket version you can carry about with you. The justification is done. Now you have to concentrate on what you have finally set down on paper. To make it more convenient, condense your goals into "Short Form". State what you "have", and some brief explanatory detail if appropriate. For example, the girl with the aircraft might say:

I have a Private Pilot's Licence and Night Rating, building up my hours and training for a Commercial. I own a Cessna 182, blue and white, fully equipped. I operate my own air taxi and charter business, and employ one pilot.

Is her goal ridiculous and impossible? It has been done! She is determined to succeed. *Are you?* Are your goals ridiculous and impossible? Will you succeed? Can you put your hand on your heart, and say with certainty, that you know where the boundary lies between possible and impossible? Have faith in yourself and the wonderful mystery of life!

Some goals will create some concern with your partner or your friends. Firstly, they might think you've gone quite silly. Well, you are an Open Person: why not allow them their opinion of you? Then they'll point out that your goals are totally inconsistent with your present lifestyle and situation. By telling people what you're up to, you invite the big hammers in. They may smash up your resolve to make a better life for yourself and those around you. When the time comes to start implementation of your goals, tell who you must. Meanwhile, keep it all to yourself.

As you were thinking and writing about your goals, did you feel that curious thrill of detachment: *being with your goals?* Did you *see* yourself as a confident, well-groomed, articulate and greatly admired person, doing the things you do best, driving away in your new Mercedes? Or waving to your sister and her husband, as your cruise ship left the quayside? Did you see it? Were you *there?*

Children daydream best. Sometimes they can invent characters that become better friends than real boys and girls. In our real dreams, have you ever wondered who some of the characters are? Where do these strangers come from, the people with real personalities, in our dreams? How can our minds invent fully developed people to inhabit our dreams, with mannerisms, tone of voice and even touch? How do we achieve such fantastic things so easily? In waking time, we often have dream-like fantasies that flash before us, when we are bored in a traffic jam, or waiting for someone. Are they real or imaginary? Our reason tells us they might be in our reality, but far from real. However, the magic of it all lends support to the reality that our wider consciousness cannot be denied. Much will be made of this later. Can you imagine yourself holding that lovely person on TV? Can you imagine yourself flying with the Red Arrows? Can you see yourself there, at the gala performance of a new film? Is the excitement of *visualisation* part of your daily routine?

You took your goals to the short-form stage. Seriously, did you or did you not *visualise the goal as being fulfilled, with you at the centre of it?* You were driving your vintage Bentley. You were able to smell the cooking from the kitchen of your own restaurant. You could see the form of your lover beside you, just as you dreamed. Well, were you, could you?

Try the "ten objects" game. Have someone select ten ordinary things from around the house. Have the items placed on the floor or table, covered up with a cloth. Ask the person to remove the cloth for ten seconds, then replace it. As fast as you can, write down the list of objects.

What methods did you use to recall the objects? Did you rely on memory alone, vision, familiarity, word retention.....or yes, *visualisation?* Your eyes have no memory, but the visual stimulus is much greater than others we have. A written list of the objects would be forgotten, even if you devised a mnemonic. A ten second visual presentation leaves an indelible impression. The vision is real; for hours, years afterwards.

The same basic process can be used to prepare elaborate visual images in our minds. A strong whiff of perfume can set a fellow's head spinning (with no woman in sight). A sudden lurch of a train is visualised as disaster and our faces pale. Nothing materially has changed, but the senses are knocked off-balance. The phenomenal process of visualisation can be extended far beyond these innocent examples. Play games with your mind! *Imagine your goals with you in them. Feel* the things you want. Experience the personal changes you want in your life. See them! *Be them!*

You now have your goals, for better, not worse. They are your goals, and you honestly want them to materialise. The goals which matter to you, are in the list. You have edited them and polished them for easy reference and recall. Now what?

After this concentrated and intense exercise, it is best to leave goals for a while, and study the process of change. Change must be understood as a powerful tool in your consciousness. Generating goals has been a serious business for you. The objective now is to learn how you will fulfil these goals. There is no goal without a purpose, and no purpose without a method. Stay with it; you are doing really well.

Eight   Everything is Change

You have your goals and the urge to do something with them. That is a significant milestone along the way. However, you may have to brace yourself for an anti-climax. Laziness, fear of the future, even fear of success, will start to creep into your thinking. Given some momentum, these feelings will convince you that the possible and the impossible are poles apart. You will see more impossibles than possibles, making you even more disheartened. In the search for absolutes, you overlook the obvious. You define goals with excitement and all the best intentions in the world, then lose sight of the dream. There is one absolute you can rely on: *change*. All your dreams are on paper *unless you will change*.

The forces within you, welcoming change, are offset by those refusing it to you. It's like swimming. Personal evolution and growth requires willing effort; become lazy and tired, and progress stops. As change waxes strong, so does the resistance. It is like having two little men inside you. One wants you to have the very best of everything; the other collects contention for you, and kicks the first little chap in the backside. Tragically, we find it easier to listen to the nasty one and obey him, than to risk change. Free will is very much connected to this basic life choice.

We learn very difficult skills over the years, and to the ones we like, we apply effort willingly. But learning the skill of arranging a better life? Now that's too difficult! If you really wanted to learn to play the piano, it would take effort, and it would demand change. A change in leisure habits, family routines and focus of interests. The changes affect you, and they affect others around you.

When you want to change your life, you are mostly changing only one person: you. It can only be assumed that your goals require changes for the better (why would it be for worse?). Certain people close to you will lend support, especially if they see the muddle you are in at present. Good supporters are precious; confiding in them sometimes will not harm you, so don't be suspicious or embarrassed. You have to accept that your wider social circle may have to change; you can safely assume you're not going to change them. Your goals may necessarily lead you away from certain people presently in your social or work life. These other people will be one of your major hurdles, if they know of your aims. Not everyone will lend support to your endeavours. They will criticise, laugh, tease, and generally block your progress. Why tell such people, especially if you know they will snigger at you? There is nothing to be gained by boasting or showing off your goals in public. In fact, it dilutes the creative energy you have mustered around you. In the privacy of your own mind, can anyone laugh at you? Why set up tiers of critics amongst your deepest desires? Every time negative people invade *your creative space,* shove them out again!

Change invites "what if" scenarios. What if I *became successful?* A better job, less self-centred, more confident? How would others feel? Would I be a stranger, a new creation? Would I have to work harder, even more pressures? If your goals are for you, then things *cannot* get worse; they can only get better. Get rid of your fear and procrastination. Your terror of failure is unbecoming to you. Stay resolute: you've come this far, haven't you?

Will you lose a piece of yourself, a piece you can't get back? Life isn't a pawn shop. Understand that you are gaining, not losing. If you give advice to someone, do you not still have the knowledge that you started with? When you show kindness, do you then have less to give to the next person? You are not dealing with finite cakes and slices here; it's more like the loaves and fishes. The more you give, the more you have to give. It's abstract, but it's wonderful. Change is not a herald for coming disaster. The popular consensus, the first instinct, is that change is to be feared. Is it a gun he has, a knife perhaps? No, it's a bunch of flowers wrapped in a paper. You have everything to gain through change, *especially change you induce for yourself.*

The process of change is subtle, but readily understood. In everything we do or experience, change is necessary to accomplish the levels of satisfaction we desire. Understanding the process is not the difficult stage by any means. *Accepting change and allowing it to happen* are the two areas which challenge us.

Having optimistic goals is the first pre-requisite. An open mind has given you these goals, and an open mind will help you to achieve them. Before this can happen, the mechanisms of change must be appreciated. There are four major steps in the change process:

Appeal to the Open Person within us
Softening the rigid attitudes.
Highlighting the current imperfections, shortcomings (not hiding them).
Creating a climate of "desirable stress".

Decision to welcome Change
Justification of replacing old with new.
Inevitability of change accepted.
Confidence in the procedure.

Input of the Goals
Visualisation of each goal when completed.
Personal relationship to goal realities.
Applying the goal requirements.

Results
Self-examination and assessment.
Feedback to review goals if necessary.
Identification with the new possibilities.

Trying to change something implies replacing the old ways with new ones. This is seldom accepted easily. We want the new, but the old must be left intact! Just in case the new way is a flop, or is too fast for us, we keep dragging the old situation about in reserve. The old ways are familiar after all, and humans do like attachments to familiar things.

The aspiring Open Person finds ways to loosen up, to soften rigid ideas, and let new ideas flood in. This causes a rise in stress level, but that is good in its own way. It puts attention on the process and generates excitement. Change is like parachute jumping: it focuses the mind, gets the adrenalin pumping, and promises thrills for those who dare.

If you don't want to change, then try to go on with yourself exactly as you are. You cannot know the pleasure of skiing if you won't go up mountains! If you're tired of the old, and look for the new, then *decide to change*. Sitting on the fence does no good in the change business. Change will push you off, however stubborn you are. Rather than ending up with bruises, consciously welcome change.

I don't like change. I see no need for most of it. For instance, they made our street one-way and now it's really awkward. We get paid bi-weekly at work now: I preferred it monthly. My boy has to change schools, because they dropped two of the subjects he wanted to take. And we can't get spares for our toaster, because the company that made it went bankrupt.

Some people sit scheming how to force changes on us. Every day in the papers, they're changing something. As soon as you understand something, it changes. Even my wife wants to change her hairstyle, and the furniture. What's wrong with our furniture? I see the clocks go back next Saturday. Why make it darker in the evenings? Is it to make the winter even longer and more depressing?

Change is happening all around me and I don't like it a bit. Everything changes, no matter how we fight it. But I have found a way to defy change. Oh yes I have! Every two years, we wallpaper our kitchen, and we've been here twenty-two years. Each time, we say we'll strip it to the plaster, but we paper on top. Everyone remarks that we've changed the paper again. But I know what's underneath; nothing has changed.

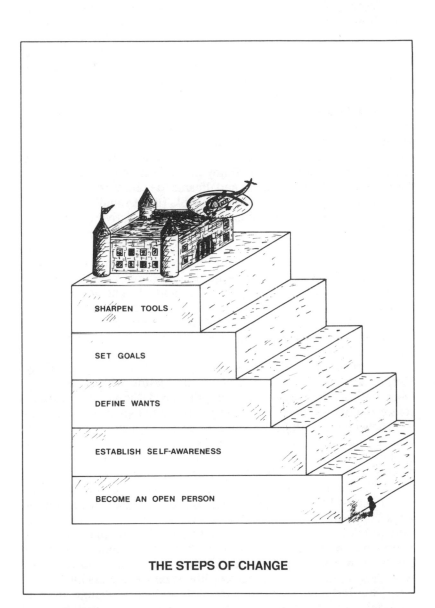

SHARPEN TOOLS

SET GOALS

DEFINE WANTS

ESTABLISH SELF-AWARENESS

BECOME AN OPEN PERSON

THE STEPS OF CHANGE

Your goals must be placed at the centre of the change process. This allows you personal control over change, which is the very thing you want. Change needs stimulation by showing your consciousness what the finished goals look like. If you want a Porsche, see the lovely thing standing there in all its glory. If it's mastering your bad temper, see yourself sitting calmly and under control, while a furious row is exploding around you.

What do you *feel like* as you are "enjoying" your accomplished goal in your mind's eye? How are you talking to people? How are you behaving? Whatever your goals, see yourself *attached to them,* and follow your own directives to the letter. Visualisation is a beautiful gift we humans have. Enjoy it, and learn to use it as a tool in the real world, to bring images and dreams to realisation.

Material goals can be highly visible in the mind's eye (that's my Porsche). Personal goals are somewhat subjective (I think I'm friendlier). You will begin to see the first changes manifesting themselves. As they do, you will feel more confident and satisfied with your efforts, further enhancing the change process as a worthwhile and exciting development. Be aware of little steps. You may wish to reconsider the priorities or specific content of your goals: that is your prerogative (isn't it wonderful you are in control?). If the Porsche hasn't come yet, that doesn't mean everything went wrong. Relax and wait. Take the steps necessary (it won't come in the next post by wishing alone).

Change begins its life as a recognition of wanting something else, or something better. We know the feeling when it happens. Once we discover ways of fulfilling this need, the process has substance. Old things look old, new things begin to look new. We appreciate how change will help us once we accept its inevitability; we can *visualise our new situations in startling detail.* Then, if we honestly apply the level of commitment required, we stimulate the change process to give us completed goals. It is really that simple.

Time is a key factor, and each person has a specific rate of assimilation to change. Don't try to have satisfied goals in a matter of weeks, or demand great leaps forward on all your goals at once. You have to learn to wait for things, and be willing to apply unfailing effort while waiting. It might take a whole year or more to adapt to the death of a family member, a divorce, or a change in location. Why should (merely) changing your life be on the express line?

Similarly, you cannot expect to suddenly change from a miserable, self-centred, opinionated and penniless drifter, to a cheerful, generous, open-minded and rich achiever! Be fair to yourself. Find your natural pace and work with it. It might be better for you to fulfil two of your goals in the next year, than to remain as you are right now. Do you think that is a reasonable timeframe for your dreams?

At this point in the proceedings, you have some insight into the preparation of goals and the nature of change. You probably feel confident that you can accomplish your goals through effort and conscious change. Given time, you will move into that wonderful state of being, where things are *really beginning to happen. You will notice a pattern unfolding. Small things, or even unrelated events, will show you that yes, there is change here!*   Remain open at all times, or you'll block forces you have summoned up.

The calling up of change is *a process of mind. It is accessed through the mind, and functions in the mind.* The rate of change is governed by factors that we ourselves promote or inhibit.

The spirit may be willing, but the old doubts creep in. The plan is there in great detail, but we bury it under layers of useless clutter. Then comes impatience, ever testy and demanding. If change was easy, just think what we could all achieve in so little time! Finding perspective on the very restricting nature of your mind, is one key in the set.

I was blasting leaves off my path with a garden hose, controlling the flow with the nozzle. It occurred to me that if I really wanted to change myself, at least, my way of thinking, the thing to do would be to stick the hose in my ear and flush out all the rubbish in my mind! If only it could be so easy! It worked so well with brittle old leaves.

I had control over the energy in the water, and the direction of the leaves. The clean path was like a new mind. Then I blasted loose gravel over the path, instead of leaves. That was interesting. I could choose what I put in my mind! I was upset when I realised the leaves and the gravel were nothing more than thoughts; they were not in control of the hose.

There is a state we can fall into, which looks very like change. It mimics the process so well, we really start believing that transformation has arrived. Unfortunately, it is hard to positively establish if change is happening. We might just be in a state of wishful thinking. (I'm *certain I've changed,* don't argue with me!). For example, someone may sit down, and write out their current situation, as part of a goal-setting exercise:

1. This job is going nowhere, nor the company. Even if it was better, I'm tired of the work and the people.

2. There's so much out there, which I'm not experiencing.

3. Several areas of my life are empty, quite unfulfilled.

4. Most people around me don't really matter to me.

5. I often question what I'm doing with my life.

6. What must happen before I make my move?

In this state of anxiety, restlessness, unhappiness, we lash out in all directions. "I'm talented! I'll show them! I have brains! I have class! I know what I want!" If we can recognise this state for what it is, then we can direct all the energy to what we want to change. Without shape and form, the steps of change are broken, loose, slippery. You will scramble about just trying to keep balance. The early stages of change always include a state of anxiety. How else will you move yourself out of apathy? Anxiety is healthy, if you know how to channel its energies into action.

Seizing the energy generated by your anxiety is good. It pushes you into new areas of self-awareness. "I really do have some control over things!" But beware. The hazards of un-disciplined zeal may catch you just at this point. When you are exhilarated by the vague promise of better things, you can fall for the wayward cousin of change: Big Mouth.

Big Mouth likes to tell everyone what he or she is *going* to do. Going to have the house in the exclusive development, the Lotus, the great career, expensive restaurants, exotic holidays at the Treetops Hotel. Eclipsing us all with infinite and exciting new talents! "I only shop for expensive clothes now. I only talk to successful people. All my projects and ideas are winners. I'm a born winner now. Yes, I've made it all happen. And you're jealous!"

All that, before Big Mouth took time to visualise goals or see if their Personal Inventory was up to scratch! No evidence either of the big step up to being an Open Person. Listen to Big Mouth. Is there any love there? Any compassion, any interest in other people? Are there qualities of honesty, sincerity, generosity, consideration for others less fortunate? Does Big Mouth take time or silence to notice what is really happening? Is the successful image of Big Mouth true success?

The energy soars and rattles the people around Big Mouth. It provides days of wishful excitement and renewed purpose. Then it dissipates, re-appearing in spasmodic bursts, but waning to a state very close to depression. How can this be? It was fascinating to track all this nervous tension speeding its way from Big Mouth's racquet. Picking up from the rebound is no fun at all. Poor Big Mouth. *You need more than that.*

Change is a quiet, purposeful thing. It is more subtle than brassy. More determined than energetic. More personal than communal. There are many counterfeit versions of change. It is well known that changing the world must begin with changing *you.* And that change process must be discrete, a private thing. So many people are blustering about, full of anxiety and noise, eager to change the world. However, little thought is spent on changing themselves. It is easier to change the whole world than to change yourself!

When you decide to affect change in your own life, please respect the process and respect yourself. Listen rather than speak. Stay open rather than assuming you have all the answers.

Change is a powerful force *within us,* which cannot abide cheap copies brought in from the external world. The voices of change are quiet, subtle, and always there if you would only listen. Stop shouting and you will hear them. When they do whisper to you, heed them, or you must set off backwards along the old path. Play games with change and you will tumble. Make it clear what you want (be *very clear*), then accept the reality of personal change. Don't allow the external world and its daily distractions to keep you from the focus you have established. It's like asking help from a good friend. If they respond in kind, take what they give you and use it.

Sharon opened her eyes and looked out from under the covers. It was Monday morning, and she was "adjusting". She enjoyed these few minutes, first thing. It was her transition from sleep to dashing about downstairs, and then rushing for the Number 29 bus.

Today, adjusting was not proceeding properly. She was four minutes over the time, six minutes. Ten minutes. That meant the next bus. She lay still, eyes wide open, tongue moistening her lips, scheming. "I'm not getting up until I know I can be a different person today", she said to the empty room. Time passed, and it meant phoning-in sick.

Her whole life played before her, like a re-run of old films when a star has died. She sighed at the sad times, giggled at others. Everything came up: all the circumstances, events, heartbreaks, recoveries. It was fascinating, lying in bed, oblivious of the outside world, watching your life projected on the wall.

The past was more bad than good, she decided. Each thing that caused her problems or pain was clearer than she had seen it before. The way she had behaved with certain people; that made her uneasy. What had she gained by being catty? The selfish attitudes, now she was on her own again....(I'll never let a man dominate my life again!). Declaring to everyone she could be anything she wanted to be. Whining over the sort of men she met, the shallow girls at work, or the dream of a BMW and charmed life slipping further into the future.

She found all the dark cellars of her life; they were all stark and frightening. She had become bored with herself, unsatisfied with her phoney ways. She could hear herself saying "Oh, what a shame, oh what a shame". In fact, she recalled saying those very words last week, without the least sincerity or compassion. But today, for herself, she meant it from the heart. She could feel tears of remorse running down her face, tears of self-pity. Then a flood of tears, a heart-clawing wail from a tormented soul, faced with the cold truth about herself. She was aware that it couldn't go on, today or any day. She hated herself.

The panic subsided and a curious calm descended. She lay thinking it was like aspirin finally taking control of a headache, or an antacid stilling an upset tummy. The bed was warm, the room quiet and safe. Ideas came into her mind. Possibilities to change herself. To start again, step by step. To deny freedom to her lower self which made life a tedious, unrewarding pilgrimage. Slowly, the prospect and the details of change entered her consciousness. It was like possessing a scrap of paper you long to find in the street, with your name on it; a note of things you must do. The secrets you crave for all your life, the directions you have sensed but ignored. It shook her with its power and its love. She had never seen things so clearly.

She stirred a little, conscious of discomfort. Her hand reached for the clock. It was half-past eight and the alarm had gone off. Twenty minutes late! She leapt from the bed and raced for the door. The sudden rush of blood made her feel dizzy and she sank to the floor. She moaned softly, and crawled back to the bed, her head throbbing.

When she pulled the covers up over her, she noticed how wet the pillow was. In a rush of knowing, the reality of her dream, the feelings, the crying, the prospect of change: it all came back. The external world was out there, yes, and she was late for it. Late for its endless and ungrateful nourishment. Today, with no guilt in her mind, she would phone in sick, and set about changing her life.

Too many people flutter about, telling you what they're *going to do*. When will they start? Others explain (at length) why they're sick of their present situation. They're bored with work, people, a cold partner, a letdown of a child, stifling routine; generally at odds with the present. The focus is on problems, not solutions. If you are at odds with the present, be very clear why. Ask yourself if you need sweeping external changes, or *internal renovation of your own attitudes*. Perhaps things are not as bleak as you think; you've just been too free with the grey paint. Once you request the power of change to act, you choose one-way. It obeys with great tenacity. Change is not a circular tour.

If you are serious about your goals, and you have allowed time to elapse to contemplate your choices, then you are ready to mobilise change. Retrace your steps to the goals you set. If everything *feels* right, you are ready. Now ask yourself:

-Have I really become an Open Person? Do I still cling to old familiar ideas, just in case?

-Have I noticed a special "closeness" to myself recently? Am I aware of what I am doing now, and how it all fits in my overall growth pattern?

-Have I identified the things in life I honestly want? Can I defend each goal openly and sincerely, against all my own probings? Are my goals genuine, and not for vain self-image or striking at old phantoms (former partner, old rivals, critics?).

-Do I have the humility to learn methods which will help me to reach my goals? Have I the essential faith in myself to persevere with the change process, which I say I want? Am I willing to give all these things daily attention for a lengthy period of time?

Change is inseparable from nature. Few people consciously acknowledge the significance of this. They say: "It's raining again today", or "It's time we had blue skies after all this rain". Are you aware of the changing seasons, the subtle changes of trees, hillsides, beaches, plants and grass, rain or shine? Do you grumble that "it's stormy", or do you watch the storm, even stand out in it, walk in it? There is nothing so humbling as a long walk in a torrential downpour, without coat or sensible shoes! At first, the elements seem spiteful, and anger wells up in us. The weather humiliates us like a piece of litter in the street. Then, as all hope of keeping dry is lost, the glorious sense of the absurd invades our minds. We can relax and accept the pounding of wind and rain! Whether you see it as bending with the wind, or rolling with the punches, changing attitude is the key to *accepting what is.*

The Open Person watches the natural processes of change, and tries to experience a closeness to it. Rather than forever running, become a partner with change. Spend a whole day, a week if you like, watching and noting evidence of change. You can't get away from it, can you? Take heart from the fact that change is part of our lives. We take in air, keep some of the oxygen, discard all the nitrogen. Every organ of our bodies is involved in change. The very humble cell (of which we have quite a few million) is constantly changing, reforming, dying. Admit it, you are a *creature of change. It is our physiology and our personal reality, every day of our lives.*

I remember you saying,
That day
Was the happiest day of your life.
Now you say you hate me:
How you change your own mind.

You concluded you loved me,
Back then;
We had discovered our place on earth.
Now we talk through lawyers:
How time can change our dreams.

I remember my saying
I'm right,
When I decided how things were so.
Now I trust the moment:
How change is all we have.

The process of change is subtle, and time is its workbench. You want change to give you things you desire. Change *gives* you those things. *These* things change. The constant casting-off need not be tragic or sad. It is only as sad as you allow. Three things are inseparable: change, time, life. What really matters is your attitude to change. Change can be used to replace attitudes, if you allow it.

We live in a state of useless worry much of the time. Good attitudes can help you to avoid uncreative stress, and organise your life more harmoniously. Some common worry examples, and their "attitude-opposites" make interesting study:

SITUATION	RESPONSE
I have a job	I worry about losing my job
I'm unemployed	I worry about not having a job
I have a job	I'm thankful for having a job
I'm unemployed	I make the very best use of my time
I have a wonderful partner	I worry that he/she will leave me
I have no partner	I worry that I'll never find someone
I have a wonderful partner	I enjoy our relationship daily
I have no partner	I enjoy life, even if I am alone
I'm healthy	I worry about being ill

I'm unhealthy	I worry about the next complication
I'm healthy	I show compassion and help the ill
I'm unhealthy	I cope with my problem cheerfully

The two attitudes say it all. Conscious change helps us to shift from one attitude to the other. Hopefully, from one of resentment and dissatisfaction, to one of accepting what is. That fundamental effort is central to your growth, and extends to the business of achieving your goals. Changing your attitudes is difficult. The majority of people grow old with attitudes they should have changed in their youth. That is how difficult it is. Only a few people take up the challenge and accept the hard work required. Are you willing to join them and live a magnificent life?

The practical application of selective change will put you where you want to be. By removing all the barriers and blocks to change, the energy can work freely. You cannot be an Open Person and resist change. Get that straight now, and forever hold your peace! By reading a book like this, you have consciously taken a step towards change. You have satisfied curiosity, but now you want to give it a try.

You might be a pessimist by nature, or beaten into passive submission by the problems and despair of the world. *Of course* we are affected by the world. The Middle East, Central America, Lebanon, Ethiopia, Northern Ireland. They all come into our lives, and we don't quite know what to do with the information. We can't write goals to solve global problems, but why don't the leaders of the world try? You are part of the problem, if you are not part of the solution. By making sense of your own situation and problems, is it not possible that the world could be a marginally better place? You might never have any direct impact against wars and disasters breaking out. But you could help the people *around you, including yourself,* to lose some of their unproductive despair for a sorry world. The place to begin is within your own consciousness.

We despair and we grumble. The world is a mess, and yes, we are a mess too. If that is your starting point (the world view of universal rock-bottom), then you have no further to fall! All you need to look for now is the optimistic voice within you, and begin to listen to it. Stop asking questions all the time. Why does a tragedy like Ethiopia happen in a world of surpluses and food piled in warehouses? Why do people go insane and shoot other citizens? Why do vandals drag our environment down by destroying things? Questions are easy; whether they are raised for world issues, or for personal crises. Senior executives often get there because they have the skill of "asking the right questions". They put others on the spot by their direct line of questions. If done in the right spirit, the questions seem participative rather than interrogative. It is akin to being a smart and resourceful lawyer. Skill in questions. But what of skill in the answers? *There is your challenge!*

You might think of changing yourself into the "type" of person you would like to be. Perhaps you like Clint Eastwood, Barbara Dickson, Madonna, or Bob Geldof. These people are fantastic as Clint Eastwood, Barbara Dickson, Madonna, and Bob Geldof, respectively. Do you think *they don't have problems?* They have no dreams, no personal qualities to improve, nothing more to do in this world?

If you mimic the image of another, you may have no more than an idealistic view of yourself: *you don't really exist as you.* Using change to build an imported self-image is dangerous, and a complete waste of energy. You must accept yourself as you are, and build on that. The bio-engineers might manage to clone your body before very long, but the idea of changing "you" into someone else is wild. *Be unique and celebrate that fact. Better to be a magnificent you than a poor reproduction of someone!*

Changing location is sometimes a promising catalyst for change (though it is by no means ideal for everyone). Moving gives you a useful shift in environment. You gain the necessary freedom to work on yourself. Your old friends are off the stage; you can act a different role (you playing you). There is considerable leverage in it. If you think it suits your goal-plan, then consider moving. Many people emigrate to other countries. They gather a few good reasons, and off they go: fed up with the weather, the quality of service, lack of opportunities. Generally, the nature of emigration allows people to operate in a pioneering spirit (impossible in a "home" environment). Each day is turned to more progress of self. This attitude adjustment of pioneering into the future is fascinating. Quite mundane, barely ambitious people stretch themselves in ways they would formerly have resisted. They become more successful both in terms of possessions and personal outreach. It could be argued that the "good life" makes it easy, so they can't fail. However, *permanent growth does occur in the individual.* The potential was always there, but environment and freshness are potent catalysts. Don't overlook this possibility.

In a macroscopic sense, things usually go well for the emigrant. The house, car, enormous fridge, the barbecue on the patio; trappings of success flow like honey from a better beehive. The *feeling* of a better lifestyle may give you more confidence, which in turn makes you attract wealth more easily. Your outward behaviour might become more generous, but the inner person may still require attention. *Location cannot alter the stuff of goals and the better life you seek; it just gives you a cleaner slate to work with.* You are the same person whether you settle in Toronto or Tobago, Tooting or Tillicoultry.

Moving to the good life can be a pipe-dream in itself, with little substance for long-term fulfilment. Unless you *seek out the right map and set of goals for your life, there is no good life, just a flight of fancy.* The good life comes from within. It is conceived within you and directed by you. Moving might help the process; it will not by itself give you what you really want. If one of your goals is to move to another country in the hope of a "better life", consider what you are taking with you. Should you leave *yourself* behind, you are rushing to be moulded into someone else's property. This time, with a different culture deciding who you are.

Change by throwing out resentment of your present situation. Be grateful for all you have. It might not be exactly what you want, but don't brood along through life; it does no good for you or your goals. If you are a naturally jealous person, always wishing for the other person's things and qualities, stop it! *You are going to get your own, aren't you?* So concentrate on that, instead of wasting precious energy.

Speak as if you are a failure, and you will become the best failure that ever was! Keep saying:

"Oh, I've never had much luck. The system's always against me. Other people get all the chances, the opportunities. My father was ordinary. I left school young, so that fixed me for all time. I'm stuck in a rut that I can't get out of. Goals are for the birds. I *know* about life".

Great! That's the spirit. Sour words (and attitudes) like that will make you a Class 1 flop!

By thinking poor, dejected and defeatist thoughts, *you attract the very things (and people) you want to avoid.* You can add to your misery by constantly discussing the terrible state of the world. Then the mess they're making with the new by-pass, declining morals, unemployment, violence, the madness of the arms race, and the price of onions. To make life grey, you have to select and serve up grey words and grey attitudes. *Change your words! Substitute bright thoughts and words in your daily life!* Keep the dark colours for funerals.

Try an observation game with people this week. Notice if anyone makes you depressed with grey news or idle gossip at someone's expense. Let people try to make you pass judgement on things. Study the words and ideas coming through. Are they happy thoughts? Do they merge into a grey commentary on everything under the sun? Can you see the words for what they are? Are they said just to kill another boring hour? What purpose can be served with grey talk? How do you react to it? Are you keeping *your* mouth of grey words shut today? Can you put a better face on things by sharing some humour, or by gently pointing out other, brighter possibilities?

Your words are your own, and they echo who you are. So are your thoughts. Why must you fashion your words and thoughts to fit in with the grey folk about you? Is it moral to be broody? Is it common decency to your fellow man, to commiserate endlessly on the horrible mess we're in? *What a shabby world we can create by merely talking!*

I was on my way to a meeting in Whitehall. I crossed the bridge from Waterloo station and came down the stairs to the Embankment. There were canvas fire hoses lying about, some connected to hydrants. Workmen were having a smoke and talking about their wives.

After the meeting, I returned the same way. The traffic was held up for some reason. I could see that the hoses were full of water; drips came from loose couplings. Under the bridge, cardboard boxes and blankets were scattered about, water flowing around them. Some boxes had been thrown from the pavement by the force of water. A dirty stream flowed by my feet to the drain.

This was hose-down day for the tramps who slept rough under the bridge. Water and disinfectant were applied at regular intervals to keep the area sanitary. It was a scene of misery. People struggled to get past on their way to appointments, in a different world. The despair could be felt by anyone who cared to look, but few did.

Across the Thames at the Royal Festival Hall, more street-people try to survive. The cardboard, pieces of plywood, and old Army blankets are there, under stairs or ramps. Yet more despair in a despairing world.

But then I noticed a man, in his late forties, sitting on a reasonably good mattress. He was eating cold baked beans from a can. The unconcerned, peaceful expression on his face made me smile. His situation was clear to all, but there was no despair in his eyes when he smiled at me in return. We were engaged in a silent appraisal of his predicament, but he was less disturbed by it than I was.

I shifted my gaze to the flamboyant, neatly-arranged poster pinned to the large cardboard box which was this fellow's February shelter. It read: THIS IS THE HOME OF MARATHON WILLIE, THREE TIMES A CHAMPION AND FIT AS A FIDDLE. WELCOME TO MY WORLD. For me, human despair was vanquished by the simple words and smile of a contented man. There he sat, eating cold beans, outside the halls where people must pay for beauty, culture, and enlightenment.

Shabbiness is a state of mind, and we all feast on it too often. We echo the thoughts of those around us, rather than take a stand. Will *you* stand up and be counted among those who prefer to be different? Will you take the risk, and see change acting in you, with advice from your little voice within?

Suicide is an easy escape when despair has no outlets, no alternatives. Yet suicide is not popular with the folks under the bridges of our world. Ending life by self-reason is more common among the middle classes, the educated and the successful. Is that not even more tragic than the despair under our bridges?

You have the choice to view this world any way you want. Perhaps your world view is immature at this point in your life. Well, let change help you to get things in perspective. You can start by discarding grey words of despair, and negative thoughts which limit both yourself and the world about you. Why *limit* the man eating his cold beans? Why *thrust despair on him?* He had an inner peace and contentment we could learn from, if only we looked beyond ourselves.

Surveys among children have shown that they see a world without hope. Kids have decided, at a very early age, that the bomb will get us, some incurable disease will drag us off, or everyday violence will do it. Short of annihilation, simply getting a job on leaving school makes the future bleak enough. They watch violent videos and they absorb grey news. Seldom do they see the *good things that are happening*. It's so rare, they don't know how to deal with it! It's "soft" or "boring". How will optimistic goals for the future appeal to them? The gloomy outlook is not restricted to children. Adults share it, often with more conviction.

My recurring theme in this book is to eliminate the concept of "impossible". Get your big broom out and sweep away your broody, defeatist self! Who said you can't do better with your life, that you'll never get out of the rut: was it you? Life is not hopeless, despite what the news throws at us. But gather grey words and thoughts into your life, and change really might be impossible.

When we decide to change, it must be a daily reality. It cannot be exclusively for work, or kept only for home life. It goes right through your consciousness in all you do. Consciousness is all you have to work with most of the time. *You are limitless, so get out there and experience limitless growth.*

Positive change is a process of faith, when you examine its roots. You don't have to be religious in any way (but note that we all have a religion, even if it's only belief in ourselves). Faith is a great and versatile reality. Its significance cannot be depreciated. If you have no faith in yourself, perhaps you don't exist! Stick a pin in your hand and then say you don't exist in space and time! We *do exist* and we do have the gift of faith inside us. Stop fighting it.

Change is a process of magic. We see magic performed, but cannot grasp how the impossible becomes the possible. We attend shows where hypnotists invite our friends up on the stage. Then we witness these familiar, rational people flailing their arms and legs about, in a hypnotised Broadway dance! They are the same people, living at the same moment, *but touched by a process of magic*. Changed beyond recognition. Even if it is under hypnosis, does it not tend to demonstrate there are significant gaps in your consciousness, which if accessed, might help you ?

If you are willing to change, you are willing to live. Why deny life to yourself? You have your chances like everyone else. The abilities you have *are* in demand, once you learn to focus them. People *do* want you to be their friend. You *can* succeed at what you have chosen to do. The higher your hopes, the better. *Lift your consciousness up* to take it all in, and wait for the results. Find security in yourself first, then work at the business in hand. Let change do what it does best: it urges the best pieces of the multi-faceted you to consolidate. The complete you is much greater than the sum of the pieces. Trust in change to show you.

Nine   The Tools in Your Hands

Without tools man is nothing, with tools he is all.

Thomas Carlyle

Imagination, if you have it, is a good start. We all like to believe we have imagination. Unfortunately, the conditioning process may have shrivelled this wonderful instrument of creativity. Too much imagination and you go insane (they say), or you live in a silly dream-like world of little practical value. Well, who has the final say? *You* have! Imagination is only one tool in your kitbag. Visualisation is another. Learning to use such tools, and becoming a craftsman, takes perseverance. But cleaning, sharpening and trusting them each day, requires love.

The tools are already inside you. Don't try looking outside, no matter what you think is out there. Your problem? You have *lost contact with the things of value within you.* Imagination is just one of them. Have you ever been amazed when sheer imagination solves a problem that wouldn't yield for you otherwise? A wild idea comes to mind. With a little modification, it fits perfectly, or sets other ideas in motion. Imagination. A powerful tool at your disposal.

The Open Person refuses to work in his own shadow. He does not block his progress by tripping himself up with every pace forward. When tools are placed in the Open Person's hands, the question is not "What am I supposed to do with these?" but "Show me how to use these to advantage". Tools are sensitive instruments made for the job at hand. Treated properly, they can help you to build wonderful things.

When we get to building our futures, and wishing we could do better in every way, there is an *impatience to get whacking at something*. If the wood is too long, you hack furiously at it with scissors or a screwdriver. That attitude will get you nowhere! Not only will you end up with savaged materials and mutilated tools, but you will be stuck where you started.

Some understanding is required before getting to work. We have been focusing on your consciousness, so let us begin there. Consciousness is an aspect of mind. Like most profound things, we seldom investigate what consciousness really is. It is the determination of reality, the knowledge of "being". It reflects the difference between illusion and reality. As thoughts and ideas arise in your mind, you recognise them. A thought without consciousness does not exist, but consciousness is always there (fortunately for us). Consciousness gives reality to your thoughts: it *is reality*. You are *really* sitting here, or standing on the bus, reading these words. Words. See? You are *reading these words! Still reading words* and now you've got the message. Is your whole reality at this moment the words on this page? Or just the present reality which will disappear if the doorbell rings? Does your entire life, and all its dimensions, find its reality in the words of this page? Or does your mind think that your present activity has nothing to do with *you* at all?

Mind is a problem. We all have one, but we seldom make any serious attempt to learn how the thing works. We study books on car maintenance, breeding tropical fish, and how the next generation of computers will change our lives. We learn the most taxing skills and adapt to incredible circumstances. But we pay marginal interest to the *very apparatus that realises all reality*.

What is your mind? Is it just a big lump of cells up there, with various lobes and fissures? Just a well-ordered hierarchy of functional zones, controlling the motor responses, vision, hearing, the senses and memory? Is the mind the anatomical unit within the skull, or the storage capacity of the brain's various compartments? Perhaps you are a left-brain (analytical) type, or a right-brain (creative) type: what does that mean in terms of *mind?* Is mind *you?* Are you really just your mind? Touch your nose. There. You obeyed! Your mind obeyed. So you are your mind. Not quite, but it's a nice theory.

It is not worthwhile to study the anatomy or the intricacies of the Central Nervous System in this context. Why understand the circuitry of a computer, if all we need is a way of using its power? At this level of study, we can get what we want, and press on.

You have three minds: Conscious, Subconscious, Overmind. The one that you know best is the Conscious Mind. That handles most of the day-to-day organisation of your life, solves basic problems, and makes decisions logically. You are using your Conscious Mind to read and disseminate the words on this page.

Next is the Subconscious Mind. Most people have heard of this one, but know very little about it. The subconscious is of interest to psychiatrists and the like, so we avoid probing too much, in case our mind goes wobbly! Negative ideas are commonly formed about the subconscious, probably because of the association with mental health. Nevertheless, the subconscious looks after us like a good grandparent. It has certain magical qualities to it as well (intuition, creativity, inspiration).

The Overmind is a projection of the Subconscious Mind, but may not be very active in most people. Telepathy and healing powers are aspects of the Overmind. The Overmind is the highest level of mind that we humans possess. People sometimes treat its faculties as a force of evil. The concepts of sixth sense, contact with the unknown, and occult connotations, appear threatening or intimidating to many people. So the Overmind is a strange one, but only if we treat it as such.

Beyond all "mind" is the Overself. This deals with things of much higher purpose. For many people, this is like a room in the house that has been locked up since the war. Now and then, a vague sense might remind us there's something of value in there. When we actively seek the spiritual aspects of our being, the Overself comes into play and becomes attuned within us. Our quest for ultimate truth goes beyond mind. A person is free to choose how far the journey goes; for our purposes here, we shall go no further than the Subconscious and Overmind.

The three minds exist together, with no natural conflicts between them, unless we stir things up. For most of the time, the Conscious and the Subconscious Minds are the ones to concentrate on. The Overmind may or may not be very "active" in you, but as it is a projection of your subconscious, I shall from this point on refer to the Subconscious Mind as including the Overmind.

It is useful to consider mind on two separate levels. This way, we can identify with the structure, and understand how the respective minds work for us. Conscious Mind is best imagined at the basal level, as it is used most commonly and directly. This is the "mind" we loosely refer to all the time. It supports the next level, the Subconscious Mind.

The Overself perches (symbolically) on top, giving energy, as it were, to everything below. Think of the Overself as the sun in your inner galaxy; it is the very essence of ultimate wisdom in your life. To draw from that wisdom, you work through the subconscious.

When we speak of mind, there is a vast area of doubt and confusion. Defining mind is like defining the concept of infinity. It is reasonable to accept this analogy, for mind can be viewed as an infinite space. Mind is not just the stuff you manage to remember, or what went in there over the years. You read a book, the facts go in. You learn to catch a fish, the knowledge goes in. You learn how to cook without burning everything, the skill is retained. You get enraged at someone, the anger goes in. It is not that simple, happily.

When things "go in", does that mean they gel up somehow and they become mind? Let's say you are really fed up today, and you decide to look inside your mind. You've never felt worse. So you find your mind, and it says you are fed up. "Hello, I'm your mind. I say you're fed up today, ha, ha!" Next day, you're up with the lark and cheerful as a sparrow. What happened to yesterday's mind? It said you were up to here with despair. It implied you were a gloomy person. Your mind has changed; it is not made of setting gel!

Psychiatrists and psychologists, behavioural scientists and genetic researchers all have their own theories on how mind develops and functions. So many experiments have been performed on animals such as monkeys, rats, dogs and of course the whale family. "Conditioned responses" might be one way to lump the features of the learning/behaviour cycle. Another approach might be based on individuality and self-esteem aspects. Animals and humans are only similar when it comes to biological and basic functioning systems. Trying to draw conclusive comparisons, and predicting behaviour by association, is somewhat dangerous. Animals conform to the excellent laws of nature, as we do. That is our common ground, and we should be proud of it. However, our faculties are multidimensional, and embrace a higher plane of awareness, discernment and potential. It may be exciting to find a dolphin showing feelings when underwater Bach is played to it. A dolphin is part of the whole, *as we are*. But could the dolphin score the music?

Humans have everything that the animals have, in basic terms. We may not be able to swim like an otter or soar like an eagle, but our form is appropriate to our experience of life. That experience can be as magnificent or as drab as we choose. We *have that choice,* whereas cows and squirrels do not. It is not even a matter of intelligence. Our minds go beyond mere intelligence. Relying on instinct and learning experiences is only one aspect of mind. Perhaps it is indeed the Overself (or whatever you may wish to call it) that separates us from the animal kingdom. Be happy that your mind is not a hollowed-out turnip full of setting gel to trap passing thoughts and feelings!

The following diagram shows the major divisions of mind. Surgery would not reveal a system so clearly defined! Yet I hope it will assist you in contemplating mind at a level we can relate to. Freud and Jung might be fascinated too.

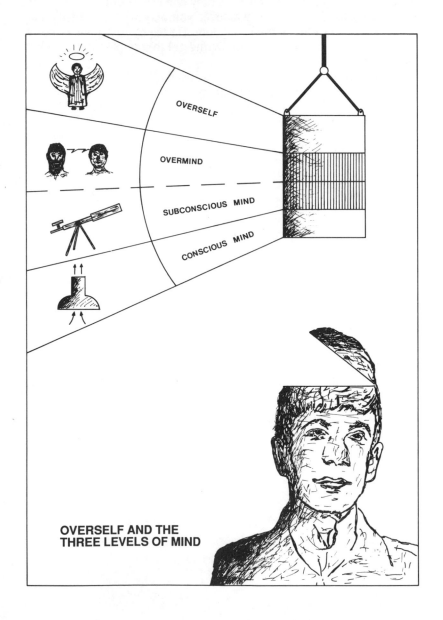

OVERSELF AND THE THREE LEVELS OF MIND

It is essential to understand the way in which mind functions in our lives. Without that understanding, you will not appreciate the power you have to change your life. The only practical way is through an example, and a diagram. The theorists of mind-definition might wince, but it might help our purposes nevertheless. We will first consider the Conscious Mind on its own.

Have you ever been in a social group, where the smokers gather at one point in the room? Have you noticed that an ashtray often sits under a table lamp? The smokers put their cigarettes there, or they wave them about under the catchment area of the lampshade. The smoke is drawn up into the mouth of the lampshade, and the filaments of smoke arrange themselves into neat, ordered patterns.

Since warm air rises, the filaments of smoke ascend through the warming effect of the lightbulb. It is fascinating to study the emerging smoke patterns at the top of the lampshade. Smoke in at the bottom, out at the top.

The warmth causes the filaments to accelerate and move through, sometimes straight and ordered, sometimes turbulent and chaotic. Filaments mix and merge with others. They collide and disperse. Once clear of the lampshade, they flow into the room, becoming diluted and undetectable. There are even occasions when smoke will travel down the outside of the lampshade and re-enter at the bottom. This gives a truly hybrid stream of old and new smoke emerging at the top.

Consider the process. Try it, if you want to see things more clearly. Use more than one cigarette. Wave them about underneath the shade. Allow calm to establish itself, and study the smooth, straight filaments of blue smoke rising from the outlet.

The lampshade and the smoke is a *model of your mind*. Watching the smoke emerging, is like watching your mind. At the bottom, thoughts, moods, emotions, ideas, desires, feelings, truths, concerns, enter the system. They are accelerated through, given a boost of energy to help them along. When they appear at the top, there they are again. If the air is still, and no mixing takes place, the thoughts and everything else emerge intact. If you could cut a slice through the "smoke" and look at it, you would see filaments like the letters in Brighton Rock. "There's anger! Look, there's fear! And there's lust!"

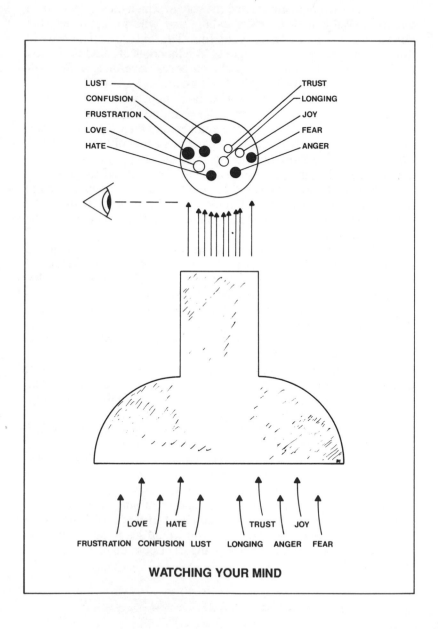

WATCHING YOUR MIND

So there you are, watching your mind at the top of a lamp-shade! By doing things with the "cigarettes" at the bottom, you can change the content of "mind" at the top. Some cigarettes might only produce "good" thoughts, so light up a few and stick them in the ashtray. Witness lots of love, joy and trust at the top. Others only produce "bad" thoughts. Light up for anger, frustration and fear. If you only light "good" cigarettes, you will most likely conclude that your life is "good" at the top end. "I'm a happy person, because I have happy thoughts". If the smoke coming out is turbulent and upset, then there must be some "bad" cigarettes there now! Of course, you can only experience one thought at a time, but alternating good and bad thoughts can emerge as quickly as you can change them.

You may perceive that you are a basically miserable person, due to watching miserable smoke coming out. That is your impression of mind, *your impression of self.* This is really an example of taking yourself too seriously, allowing "self" to confuse miserable thoughts with the essential "you". Your Conscious Mind is a *thought factory:* there are gloomy Monday thoughts, and happy Friday ones. Neither day's thoughts can claim to be *you,* but of course they do affect your approach to life. When a jolly thought comes up, you might find fault with it (judgemental position). "No jolly thoughts here, I'm trying to be miserable! My mind is full of miserable thoughts, so I cannot tolerate happy ones!" The fascinating thing to grasp among the smoke is that you have some control over your own thoughts. Thought-discipline is a difficult skill to acquire, but if you become disenchanted with miserable thoughts, start consciously thinking happy ones!

To understand our minds, we need more than just a lampshade and a packet of cigarettes. The central issue is there, nonetheless: *are those thoughts you, or are they just thoughts?* How should our consciousness relate to thoughts? Think about peeling potatoes with a sharp knife. The inevitable happens: you cut yourself. Think about the panicky feeling as you study the cut, waiting for the blood to stream out. Aaaggh! Not a pleasant thought, was it? But have you become an unpleasant person all of a sudden, or a person scared to handle kitchen knives again?

Thoughts come and go. We listen to someone nearby moaning away in vivid detail. Thoughts come into our mind. "Why doesn't he shut up? Monday again. This train is dirty. Oh give us a break. There's an apple core. I think I'm sweating. Too much trouble in the world, I agree. That guy looks nice. I like my new blue shoes. Chewing gum. My stop next. I'll have a cheese roll at 11".

The Conscious Mind is a chatterbox; something like a hyperactive child after two bags of sugar. It is both a marvel and a pain in the neck. It rattles on, talking to itself, creating problems, solving problems. It *pretends to be you,* but it knows it isn't.

"Hello, I'm your mind! Is there anybody out there, in here? This is *you* talking. Can't you hear me talking to you? You talking to me? I know all you know, and more besides. I can remember things, can you? But I am you! I am your memory, your thoughts and your everything! I am your past and your future! Hello, this is your mind. Hello. Hello!"

Your Conscious Mind must be kept in its place. It is a wonderful thing to be in possession of, but there is no need to follow every little game it decides to play with you. Your Conscious Mind is like a rabbit. It hears a noise and it's off. It thinks it hears another noise, and it scuttles off down a burrow. It overhears another rabbit: there might be hunters out today. So everything that happens today is all hunters and guns. Don't be fooled by the amazing utility of your Conscious Mind!

There is a tendency to entertain problems *using only the Conscious Mind.* This is rational enough, at least to get started. Gathering the facts, analysing them, then acting on a decision is sensible logic. The bigger the problem though, the more data we heap on. Analysis is the bread-and-butter of the Conscious Mind, and it gets to work analysing. Aware that the analysis might get bogged down for want of information, it tells us to gather yet more data for it to analyse. Rather than facing up to the problem, admitting the worst and accepting it, we play games with data in our Conscious Mind. Procrastination and avoidance never solves problems, nor helps us to plan our lives constructively.

Experts solve "big" problems by searching databases, conducting studies, and retaining consultants who give objective appraisals of alternatives. Where computers are used, solutions are assumed to be as right as solutions can possibly be. We load data which is right, so the solutions and the output scenarios must be right.

By winding our expert faculties up to twanging point, we assume that the right "key" has been reached to play the music. Brainstorming brings out the alternatives, but the decisions drive us to exhaustion. In such cases, people are definitely not operating on *the basis of hunches.* They are relying on pure and simple reason, and knowledge of the relevant facts. Beyond that, the processes of the Conscious Mind are mechanically applied to the exercise. Computers or consultants apart, the problems are tackled by the Conscious Mind.

The more complex the issue or the problem, the more data is collected and the more consultants hired. More and more computer time is spent on data reduction and trend analysis. Hopefully, something drops out of the machine. The data, facts, trends, patterns: all lead to a call for action. A commissioned study may lead to sweeping changes, implemented to the letter. Or it may be shelved as inappropriate, because the Managing Director *likes to try his hunch* rather than the massed Conscious Minds of his troops.

When we tackle our life problems and our goals, we seldom have the vast resources of corporate databases or consultants! The problems they are trying to wrestle with are usually different in any case. The Conscious Mind, and the exercise of reason, are only ideal for certain types of problem.

We often worry ourselves into states of high anxiety over personal problem-solving. In fact, much of the character disorders and neuroses of our modern society stem from denying that problems exist, or refusing to deal with them at all. We leave the problem unsolved, but create a worse problem by becoming neurotic! Sometimes the effects of our clumsy approaches to a problem are just as damaging. We certainly cannot use methods used in the business world. *We need an even better system.*

This leaves us with the other mind of interest: the Subconscious Mind. What can it do for us? What power does it have? We could say that the subconscious is a medium for wisdom, although it is not wisdom itself. Wisdom is nothing like knowledge. Your Conscious Mind rattles along all day, dealing with knowledge in the form of thoughts, and preparing thought groupings for memory. Facts, facts, facts. But where is the wisdom? Conscious Mind is aware of itself, always proving its worth. Subconscious Mind *just is;* it doesn't question everything, but does what it does very well. The real chance of making sense of knowledge lies within the Subconscious Mind. It is always at your disposal, twenty-four hours a day. But unless it is given instructions, it just plays second fiddle to your Conscious Mind.

Dreaming takes place in the subconscious. At that level of consciousness, you may fly above a city without an aircraft; suddenly find yourself talking to the Queen; or experience bizarre episodes with steam trains, soldiers in the streets, and you in your underwear. Despite the seemingly haphazard images of your dreaming mind, the analysis of certain significant events tells a psychiatrist (and you) a great deal. Awake or asleep, your Subconscious Mind sees you as you really are, without disguises. Viewing yourself only with the Conscious Mind may be very limiting, or too flattering. Your subconscious knows you best.

We learn as we go, and there's a lot of knowledge already in there now. Brainy people believe they know it all. They try to impress the rest of us, struggling to understand the basics. Talk to a scientist: he will view the world and his life in generally scientific, functional terms. A Paris pavement artist with talent, poverty and dreams, thinks he knows how things really are. Both are victims, not wizards, of their learning. Each has a personal world view, but there is nothing to say that either has wisdom. Their knowledge is nothing close to wisdom. Neither wisdom of reality, nor wisdom of themselves.

The knowledge and the learning we stuff into ourselves becomes a handicap in many ways. It tends to overwhelm and ridicule any other forms of consciousness. Our world view (based on our learning and our progressive conditioning) may tell us the world is a horrible place. Ideas to improve one tiny aspect of it then become absurd to us. "No room for silly, soft ideas here!" *Don't rely on all that knowledge inside you.* It might be impressive at cocktail parties or in your learned circles, but give it only nodding respect.

Your Subconscious Mind is your *gateway to insight, intuition and real wisdom.* It is your friend, your mindful guardian. It warns you of danger and helps you through difficult times. It is a *magic force within you, available and willing to help, always. Whatever honest goal you assemble in your Conscious Mind, the Subconscious Mind can help you to achieve it, solve it, or create it.* The Subconscious Mind never goes to sleep, nor does it ignore you if it gets tired (it never gets tired). Ask it for something, and it *listens.* Your Conscious Mind is good at puzzles and IQ tests, but try asking it to really help you! Since your subconscious is watching over events, it is *taking note of what you are doing right now.* Perhaps it was your Subconscious Mind that instructed you to buy this book and get started on your new life!

There is nothing new in this. Nothing strange or threatening either. *People who take charge of their lives learn to access their Subconscious Mind.* They discover the practical value of a focused life, accessing real wisdom instead of facts, figures, idle thoughts and elusive states of Conscious Mind. They learn to see the world and their place in it rather differently. *You can do the same thing.*

You have energies and powers you unconsciously subdued over the years. The conditioning processes, from learning how to use the toilet properly, to preparing yourself for an interview, have forced "unusual" practices out. You must rediscover the very things you were urged to remove. Integrating abstract concepts into your everyday routine is far from easy, but then nothing worthwhile ever is.

Access to the subconscious allows us to gainfully harmonise the two levels of mind directly available to us. It is something like the ability to recall "interesting" dreams at will. How often have we been frustrated by whispers from fascinating dream-voyages, lost forever in the subconscious, memory unable to trace the thread? We can do great things in our dreams. The waking state has too many restrictions. When the Conscious and Subconscious Minds work together, with mutual respect for each other, the phenomenon of a "new person" transformation becomes possible. Serendipity then enters the picture in a new, exciting way. Rather than "other people" having "all the luck", we begin to see that serendipity is available to all, but only if we reach out and make use of it. The subconscious knows serendipity well; your Conscious Mind does not.

The subconscious has a negative aspect, which should be explained at this point. Just as the Subconscious Mind desires to be your guide and inner strength, it also has the capacity for frustrating and actually harming you. Since it has no reasoning ability of its own, it is apt to treat all incoming messages as equal entities. Thus, if your boss or teacher dresses you down in a passionate tantrum of criticism, the subconscious assumes it's all true! If your self-esteem and Conscious Mind are off guard, you store the message deep in your subconscious. An unconscious feeling of inadequacy is created. So many of our phobias, hidden fears and personality problems stem from this aberration. Just as we can implant positive suggestions, we can also cultivate negative ones.

Awareness of this leads to a precious truth. If we can replace "wrong" themes in our subconscious with "right" themes, we can look forward to better lives in every way. Learning how to direct the childlike, unquestioning nature of the subconscious is essential. The Conscious Mind will guide you in that task.

Sceptical people will find this all quite absurd. They will say you are absurd (behind your back)! *Everything* is absurd to some people (not you I hope). They have no belief or faith in anything other than cold reality, hard facts, and perpetual analysis in the Conscious Mind. *Stop listening to them. Listen to yourself.*

How can you listen to yourself? Now that really is absurd! Voices from the beyond perhaps? First of all, *believe in belief,* as a practical concept of growth consciousness. Believe that what you need is inside you, and you will learn how to access it. No voice will physically speak, but the information you need *will be decanted into your Conscious Mind* for you to act upon. The Subconscious Mind carefully assembles the *right guidance* and the Conscious Mind acts as an interface with you. You can readily perceive the Conscious Mind. The subconscious is hidden out of the present and must be accessed by protocol. Learning the basics of that protocol is the task at hand; there is no other way to the wisdom you require.

The best place to listen, is in a quiet environment. Real silence is a luxury that eludes us, unless we consciously stop the noise we and others create. Many people avoid the uncanny atmosphere of silence and solitude. It worries them, threatens them. They must be around active people, TV and hi-fi's. They *must* speak, feeling that silence in company signifies dis-approval, perhaps a hint of finding others shallow. They allow torrents of noise to destroy their peace; they talk for hours with no particular focus or purpose, with no real communication. Noise, constant noise, like a radio frequency badly tuned; irritating, distracting, unproductive. Real silence and solitude is essential for the Subconscious Mind to function. It is a sad reality of our society and civilisation that we act as if we are working to escape from ourselves. Why do that, or allow others to lead you so?

You can find silence in a quiet room (with no chance of disturbance). Silence abounds on hill-tops, deserted beaches, or in caves. Sitting in a rowing boat out on a lake is an excellent place of silence (assuming the water-skiers have gone). Early morning, even in the heart of a city. Silence. Frightening to some. Self-challenging, intimate. If you are going to make progress, *you must find a silent space to go to.* Earplugs might be sufficient if your neighbours like to share their noise.

Find your silent place and go to it as often as you can. You should try to have some truly silent time every day, even twenty minutes in a relaxing bath. You must not have a radio or other distraction at your side. The whole point of silence is to be utterly alone with the little ears and voices inside your Subconscious Mind. They will not make the effort to communicate with you if you're tapping your toes to some other beat.

Just in case you're wondering what you are getting wound up for, I should be open with you. It's essentially meditation. (But no incense, candles or chanting!). Meditation is a well-established means

of settling your Conscious Mind and moving through to the higher
levels. It might sound weird to you if you've never meditated before.
But then you did say you were an Open Person now.

SILENCE AND THE SUBCONSCIOUS

This exercise introduces practical methods which will help you re-establish contact with your own subconscious. You must be in a silent environment, with no chance of casual disturbance. Pressures of time and everyday concerns must be absent.

SILENCE

Sit on a chair, on the floor, or upright in bed, keeping your spine straight. You don't have to be a Yoga Master, just be relaxed. Immerse yourself in the quiet of the room. Be aware of your inner doubts, and the fact you are doing this peculiar thing. Look about you, and carefully study each familiar thing that your gaze rests upon. Let the usual pattern of thoughts carry on as before. Don't worry that you're not taking this seriously enough. Your Conscious Mind loves new things. It's having a new experience, and it wants to have a running commentary on this funny thing you're doing. All the while, try to lose focus on strong, dominating thoughts: treat them with courtesy, but don't let them chatter at you.

Your Conscious Mind will be highly excited at first. As you adjust to the environment of calm, the Conscious Mind will slow down somewhat. After some minutes, begin sensing your breathing. Breathe in, breathe out, breathe in, breathe out. Deep, slow breaths. Keep your attention fixed on your own breath. Feel it entering and leaving your body. Sense the physical and auditory sensations as it passes through your nostrils or your mouth. Feel your chest rising and falling in sympathy. Your silent space, your breath, your life. Thoughts will float about, but return your focus to the breathing process. Simplicity, vital simplicity. Imagine that each breath calms you down more and more.

After a few minutes, divert your attention to your eyes. Keeping your head horizontal, roll the eyes upwards, trying to gaze through your eyebrows. Blink *only if you must*. Your eyelids will become progressively tired, and you will want to close your eyes. They may open, so look up as before. Eventually your eyes will close. Opening them will seem like too much effort, too much bother. This voluntary submission will relax your entire body. Don't fight the relaxation, simply enjoy it. Settle down comfortably. Don't go to sleep though. Allow yourself to drift into a state of quiet but conscious relaxation. Study the little thoughts streaking through your mind like smoke filaments from a lampshade. Look at the thoughts as they drift up; then allow them to disperse into the room. Quiet time. Alone with yourself. A good time. Helpful, encouraging. Nothing weird about this, it's interesting, uplifting, magical. You are meditating.

Adjustment to the silence varies from person to person. There is no right or wrong way to reach a state of calm well-being. If you consciously try to fight the process, you'll never get very far into it. If your mind is in a cynical, doubting, self-defeating mode, you may have to try again later. Allow time for the smoke to clear! Your thoughts may all be bad today! Your first sessions may seem a waste of time, but at least they prepare you for better. Don't give up. This isn't an easy thing you're doing. Attitude, belief and tenacity are essential.

By shutting out the chatter and gossip of the Conscious Mind, it is possible to hear the inner voices, "whispers", from the subconscious. Conversely, your subconscious will be able to *hear you.* It is as simple as that. The *listening effort* is the skill to grasp here, not some trick of raiding inspired thoughts from the deep. Your Conscious Mind (in the form of your ego) will be teasing you and laughing at you whenever you go to meditate. Persevere. You are *not* your Conscious Mind!

On this exercise, you are not looking for any great manifestations from your subconscious. You are merely trying to experience what silence and self-contact really is. No doubt, you will notice curiosity building up in yourself, an urge to go further next time. There is a pleasant calm and strength in "listening to the silence". It seems to achieve nothing on the face of it. But patiently, respectfully stay open to *what you see and feel in that silent space.* Everything is relevant. Even the trashy thoughts that whizz about; the noises you may hear outside. The fascinating sounds of your own breath hissing to and fro as you contemplate your silence.

DEEP SILENCE

This is simply a more developed state which follows the silence and relaxation established earlier. It needs only time and continuing calm to come about. Here, you will have managed to put your Conscious Mind into neutral for most of the time. Odd thoughts will come and go. Some will linger, asking for attention. Old worries, old amusements, old friends, old enemies. Reminders about you sitting there doing this very funny thing. Give them a respectful wave and see them on their way. At this stage, you will witness your thoughts as having much less impact on your overall present-consciousness. In fact, this is a simple confirmation of having reached deep silence through straightforward meditation. You will also experience a feeling of well-being, a comfortable state between blissful sleep and focused awareness.

In deep silence, your attention finds your breathing much more interesting than anything in the mind. Thoughts still come and go, but they cannot drag your attention away from the breath for very long. Each time you do scamper off like a rabbit, effortlessly come back to the fascination of your own breath.

A deeper calm will arrive for you. Random thoughts are less interesting and less intrusive at this point. You consciously begin to *ignore your own random thoughts!* They cannot command your interest any longer! You have your thoughts but they don't have you! This deeper calm *approximates to a trance state induced through self-hypnosis.* If the doorbell rang, you'd be quite aware. Don't feel anxious about losing control. The hypnotic state is under your direction: you are the master and the subject. You cannot become hung-up in this state: the natural tendency is to come out of hypnosis or simply snooze and then wake up.

Mere thoughts are secondary to a *greater awareness* you have created for yourself. You are aware of your breath, aware of yourself, and generally much less focused on thoughts forever moving about. You begin to revel in the silence. You might find yourself patting yourself on the back and saying how smart you are. But that is your Conscious Mind (ego) slipping a little vain thought in! You recognised it as such, and back you go to the calm again. Not only do you have calm; *you have control.*

It is in this wonderful state of calm that we can *watch the mind.* Just as you imagined you were watching "mind" when observing smoke going through a lampshade, here you are *conscious* of watching the vast open space of your actual mind. You have put thoughts where thoughts belong. You appreciate mind for what it is. It is less threatening to you now, less intimidating, less limiting. It doesn't throw worries or anxieties at you, like old hob-nailed boots. It doesn't demand undivided attention to the relentless internal dialogues going on between factions of Conscious Mind. *Rather than losing your mind, you have found it!*

SILENCE AND THE SUBCONSCIOUS MIND

The Subconscious Mind is *available to you* at this stage. The Conscious Mind is there alright, but in a safe state of calm. It has become sluggish in manufacturing thoughts. It no longer has the energy to fire thoughts into the general consciousness, like a child thrusting toys at you, wanting to play. In fact, the Conscious Mind is rather *enjoying* this little break you have given it. (This is how many burnt-out people regain balance: they need to give their Conscious Minds some rest and recreation).

In this very deep state of relaxation and inner calm, you may begin to feel a certain elation, beyond the possibilities of mere definition by the Conscious Mind. The feeling of calm develops into one of *ultimate trust in yourself.* You are understanding what it *really* means to be an Open Person. You are in touch with yourself. The little ears and voices of your Subconscious Mind are waiting for you now. There are no Sony Walkmans, no booming televisions, no pile-drivers or telephones. No people talking at you, no thoughts jumping around like children on a trampoline. Don't fret that you are unable to experience "visions" or paranormal events, nor any particular feeling that you are different in some way. Nothing startling should happen: it's really a very ordinary, unspectacular process. *But it's important.*

Coming out of a session is easy. Rather than immediately rising as if nothing had happened, follow a procedure that suits you. For example, think to yourself "That was a good session; next time will be even better. I'm nicely relaxed, refreshed. I feel good. When I open my eyes, I'll be recharged, calm and happy". Smile, and resume your chores of the day.

GOALS AND THE SUBCONSCIOUS

The gentle Subconscious Mind, with its potential for communication with you, is there all the time. How can the safebreaker hear the soft clicks of the combination lock, if there's a brass band in the vault with him? Similarly, how can you attune to the help available in your own subconscious, if your "mind" is clacking away saying "Here I am, here I am, am I not wonderful, here's some more thoughts and worries to clog you up"?

Talking and relating to your Subconscious Mind is the very process by which you can make some sense of your mind and your life. The wisdom is in there, if you can be bothered to listen for the soft clicks of the lock. Visit your Subconscious Mind a few times before asking things of it. Do you borrow things from new neighbours as soon as you meet them? Show some respect! You may have to practise many times before feeling "this is right". Familiarity and patience will help. Eventually you will reach the desired state of calm in a matter of five minutes (or less). You may feel that you have not achieved the "depth" required. Actually, you will be surprised how little depth is enough.

Now you have some ideas on the technique of accessing your Subconscious Mind. It is necessary to learn the best ways in which you can approach it and ask for help. Meanwhile, it is imperative that you become familiar with silence, and the workings of your two minds. Don't just accept what you are being told. Seek it out for yourself, prove it, and continue to believe in it. In this regard, practice the meditation exercises until they become part of your daily activities. Consider them to be just as vital to your well-being as good food and exercise. Learn to enjoy these sessions. Look forward to them. Never consider them as intrusions on your time or sanity. Don't treat them as a peculiar experiment that you are merely observing with your ego!

You can bring out your goals now. Interesting as it might be, the study of mind is not the purpose of this book. The immediate application of your Subconscious Mind is in the area of achieving goals, which you have set for yourself. While you were researching and preparing your goals, your subconscious was well aware of what you were about. (The Conscious Mind was giving its usual commentary).

Assemble your goals, and become intimately familiar with them. If you have too many, limit them to a number you can cope with. You have been through the mind-exercises of visualising your goals, before and after they were in finished form. In a subtle way, you have already introduced the goals that matter to your Subconscious Mind, via the analytical Conscious Mind. So you need not worry that all this is going to be a shock to the system. In fact, your subconscious may have helped you to select your goals, fleshing out the good ones from the chaff. You may not have been aware of its silent urging.

Visualise your goals whenever you have a day-dreaming moment. Don't wait until you meditate. It keeps the goals fresh in your consciousness, so you are always aware of what you are wanting to do. The achievement of goals is a *constant sport of mind,* so keep the ball in play. Visualisation is best for the subconscious: a picture has more meaning than pages of words.

When you have a meditation session, you can take one of your goals in with you. That doesn't mean reading out the entire goal to your subconscious, saying "OK, that's it. I want this by 5 o'clock on Thursday". Have the content of the goal in short-form, easily remembered and visualised. Special words don't have to be prepared for your subconscious. It knows what you mean. The substance of the goals will be clear enough, without elaborate, patronising words. If you know what you mean, why would your own subconscious need special language? Single words will often be enough to suggest what you mean. Visual translations will then take over.

Once you have completely established your deep silence, *make your Subconscious Mind aware of the goals you want to see fulfilled.* No need for explanations, just *consciously think the goals in there and leave them alone.* Make a routine of it.

Every time you have a session, review your goals beforehand, and offer them up during the session. You are simply consulting with your own Subconscious Mind, to jointly manage the business of realising goals. The only requirement is that the consultation be carried out in a state of inner calm. Your subconscious always respects your attention to such details of protocol, and will reward you with results.

If you have prepared beforehand, the goals will be fresh in your memory. They never have to be word-perfect, just clear. A clear visual image is better still, if you are good at calling up images in this way. Tell it to your subconscious; share the problem or the dream. Then visualise the goal in its finished form (during the meditation), just as you have done in its preparation.

You might think it ridiculous to say "I have a Jaguar XJS Convertible, white with red seats". Material goals are not in the present reality, although I urged you to state them this way. That is the problem of dealing with the new while the old is still firmly in place. With personal goals, there is no problem: self-suggestion impresses the subconscious, displacing negative themes you had collected. Material goals need some additional care.

Visualise the completed material goal as *a consequence of definition, a reality which you are attaining with the help of your subconscious*. As explained earlier, the subconscious tends to accept messages as gospel. Learn to harmonise the Conscious Mind to your meditation (preparation and post-session). You can use both minds to make sense of the anomaly; project the material goal in such a way that the subconscious realises the XJS has still to be found!

Your point of focus is your own Subconscious Mind hearing your own goals. Once the goals have been shared, there is nothing more to do but wait. Some of the things you have asked are not straightforward. These will require time. But be careful. The subconscious has a very poor sense of time. Your Conscious Mind is the one watching the clock. Both minds have to become synchronised: if you don't specify some form of schedule, you might get what you want, but much too late! You will have to use the Conscious Mind to "pace" requests and directives concerning the subconscious.

Your Subconscious Mind will be aware of what you want, and *will begin looking for opportunities on your behalf. When there is something that will help you, the Subconscious Mind will lead you right to it. It will also make you open and focused enough to see possibilities beyond your immediate perception.* It will not be obvious at first, especially if you are unaware of the process taking place. Apply yourself to the silence from which all these things grow.

You may already appreciate that meditation can be used to establish inner calm and promote a sense of wholeness. If there are opportunities for you to join a meditation group, by all means join it. You don't have to be the "type" to do such things. Where is the Open Person now? Meditation is a singularly powerful tool in the understanding of mind, and the potential levels of consciousness that we humans have. *And that means all humans, not just fortunate ones.*

The meditation method used here is structured around achieving results. There is no attempt at realising higher, spiritual things. Nevertheless, it trains you in the *discipline of mindfulness*. It gives you a focus point you perhaps never thought existed. When you become aware of yourself in this special way, the impossible is more and more possible. For a change, the mind becomes a *listening* entity, rather than a *chattering* one.

By willingly sharing your goals with those little ears beyond the gossip, you get the support, the advice, and the guidance you need to achieve your goals.

During and after meditation, *certain clarifications* will surface. Strong urgings will direct you in particular ways, when the time is right. You may receive powerful, conscious thoughts which suggest alternatives, or fresh insights. Direct commands may come: "Go and build your house....you can do it....the money is not an issue". Some sessions will appear to produce nothing. The time is not ripe. Then one day in the garden, or in a crowded shop, the idea pops! Your Subconscious Mind never sleeps, remember? Don't expect a one, two, three directive to achieve every goal. Remain flexible and let things work out as they will. The actual form of manifestation will vary from person to person.

When you begin to sense the feedback from your subconscious, don't get haughty and decide "you" know better. You know better than the deep wisdom accessed through your subconscious? If that is where you are, go back to "The Open Person" and give yourself a second chance! Signals, help, advice and instructions from your Subconscious Mind are there for you to use. Exercise discretion to defer action, if sudden application of the directive would be inappropriate. But don't snub your own subconscious by deferring all the directives! Don't try modifying or conditioning the ideas. Why condition messages when you sought unconditioned help in the first place?

Throughout the practice of communicating with your Subconscious Mind, you must continue with some less heady exercises:

-Read your list of goals out loud to yourself every day. Read them slowly, deliberately, and learn them by heart for your meditations. As you read them, imagine you are already with your goals. See them, feel them, visualise them completely finished.

-See yourself as the person you want to be. Go about each day as if you *are* the person. It sounds like acting a role, but it's a dress rehearsal for the person you are growing into. Take this exercise seriously.

-Before you meditate, have your goals ready in your Conscious Mind. Take a moment to impress your consciousness with the business at hand. It makes life easier for you in the middle of a wonderfully calm and productive session.

You know that your Subconscious Mind works. How often have you had a problem with several variables to tease you, and the answer just refuses to come? Then you consciously *forget* about the problem, from frustration or spite. Suddenly, at the least likely time, up pops the answer! It can be startling enough to make you laugh at yourself. We draw on the subconscious without even knowing it. Sometimes, the results have us convinced we have nothing short of a miracle on our hands. Just imagine the feeling if we could learn how to develop this tool properly, and use it every day! The sceptics declare it's all coincidence. Allow them that; but results are what you want, not judgements.

If your goals are real and reasonable to you, they will be real and reasonable to both levels of your mind. You must then work with your Subconscious Mind in the proper way: in silence. Gentle coaxing begins the process; respectful attention to the promptings completes it. That is the way to realise your true capabilities.

Present yourself and your goals to your Subconscious Mind, in the silence of meditation. You will increasingly see the sense of what you are doing. You will be closer to the real you than ever before in your life. When the "little voices" give you the clues and the directives, heed them. You are on your way. Faith is not just believing what you know to be untrue. It is a tool and you must respect it. Respect yourself, and what you are doing.

Part IV

What is missing? Are you ready for success?

"I've got problems, underneath the surface. Maybe we all need psychotherapy. But digging all that junk out would spoil everything for me".

"A goal to travel to China is realistic; accepting my son's drug addiction is absurd, even if he is reformed now".

"It's all too good to be true. I follow the arguments, but I'll drift along thankyou".

"There must be more to life, yes, I've always felt that. But you know the problem? It's fear of yourself and what people think".

Ten   The Goals You Avoided

There must have been goals you discarded as ridiculous or trivial. No doubt you weeded out those that made the list look greedy or unmanageable. How can a person focus on twenty or thirty goals? Even ten goals can make you very busy. If your list is absolutely complete, you are either a truly Open Person, or you are prone to deceiving yourself.

You never thought that setting goals had anything to do with taking skeletons out of cupboards, did you? One possible reason you missed some goals: fear of other people seeing them. Another: *you do not want to see them.*

What goals could these be? How about overcoming a roguish temper, wanting to give money to a good cause, re-aligning yourself with abandoned or rejected spiritual beliefs, reconciling yourself with a wayward daughter or a bullying father?

Then there are the sexual ones. Secretly wanting to let go. The confidence to discuss things openly with a partner rather than bottling up fears and frustrations. To feel uninhibited when exchanging ideas on technique. To dispel the stereotypes of male/female roles and myths in order to be sexually mature.

There may be things in your past that haunt you. Your forgotten goal might be to think it all through and reach a better understanding or solution. Perhaps the issue needs consultation with a psychotherapist, but your goal could be to explore the problem on your own first. Avoiding the problem creates more complex problems. Why have all the trappings of the good life, but suffer misery from neuroses?

You may have taboo goals related to very low self-esteem, or personal inadequacy. You might have decided, in some anguish, that you need a nose or an ear job. But then, that's too expensive (or silly). People would laugh. People laugh when you have a funny nose; they laugh after it's fixed. That's people! Where does low self-esteem come from? Well, other people play their part, but so does your chattering mind. In any case, if you feel a shapelier nose would help you, then it's a goal, so waste no time in declaring it a goal!

Relationships and matchmaking is an area of concern for many. This is a complex area, of interest to married couples and long-term lovers, as well as lonely hearts. Too many people just drift, experiencing a vague sense of dissatisfaction with a current relationship, or the loneliness of being a single in a couples' world. They think the perfect combination will "happen" one day, but are frustrated when it never does. It is very much a case of sights being set too high, or conversely, acting before thinking at all. Both courses lead to trouble. The well known "married at 23, divorced at 33" cycle shows that people traditionally satisfy social and ego pressures before determining what they really want from life. Although a formalised relationship was "right at the time", people often blossom as individuals *after separating*. Everyone not already settled in the "perfect relationship" generally wants to meet the ideal soulmate, unless they have consciously opted to be independent (and there's nothing whatsoever wrong with that). There is an element of self-motivated destiny in meeting the *right* one, rather than *one that will do!* The best partnerships then generally evolve from mutual attraction, *shared values* and a growing state of harmony. Write a goal to achieve the relationship you dream of: "I want a loving, committed relationship in my life, with the person I know is right for me".

Then there are goals which *shoot themselves.* "*My* problem is too big to be solved". Oh yes? The can't-get-there-from-here syndrome. Another one is the hard-luck, dedicated martyr. "I really want to get out of the rat race and live off the land in Mull, but my wife hates hardship and my two kids are happy in their school. I see my life as a prison now, and there's no pardons in this world...." The next type is the diametric dreamer, always wanting to prove the world wrong. "You say you can show me how to run my own airline like Richard Branson, but you damned well know I'm only a butcher from Wakefield and all I can do is saw chops". The Possible versus the Impossible. Don't keep painting yourself into corners by being either too humble, or excessively ambitious.

Why not get your goal roughly sorted out, no matter how confused you are? Then, if it's appropriate, talk to your confidante, without being too specific at first. That family might find Mull ideal:

they might welcome Daddy leading them out of the rat race and chain stores. We all get trapped in our collective roles. Remember, if you haven't a proposition, you can't mull it over, or expect a response.

One other goal form that causes people some concern, is the "if only" variety. If only you *had done* or *did not do* something. Mistakes made in the past are long gone, washed out to sea, dissolved to ions. However, we love to keep them with us "for balance". There are many other problematic goals. Here's a synopsis of topics for your immediate reference:

Excessive Personality or Behaviour
- Control of anger and violence
- Abrasive characteristics
- Self-persecution, including self-inflicted anxiety
- Hyperactivity leading to burnout

Relationships
- Splitting up with a partner
- Resolve to avoid breakdown
- Containment or grounding of animosities

Spiritual
- Answering call to higher purposes
- Lack of information, unaware of facts
- Pressures of popular opinion, consensus
- Fear, guilt, mis-conceptions, irrational ideas

Reconciliatory
- Parental, children (past unpleasantness)
- Friends or business partners (betrayal, conflict)
- Parties to accidents or tragic experiences

Disapproval of Material Goals
- Partner or family causing guilt complex
- Extravagance with no responsibility

RECONCILIATION

Background

My wife had an affair with a man she knew at her work. I couldn't understand why at the time: we had everything going for us. We were finally seeing returns for all the hard work we put into our home, and overcoming various setbacks together. I could sense she had been out in the afternoons, but to challenge her seemed pointless. I didn't want to know the truth, I suppose. When I noticed more positive signs, I decided to set the trap. It was easy. It seemed peculiar, funny almost, seeing another man in your bed with your wife. No drama though, just an escape to think. We separated for a year (the affair collapsed after three weeks). Now she wants to begin again. I've taken all this very well, but deep down, she broke my spirit. But then, I see her fling as a comedy of errors, rather than a kick in the teeth. Part of me wants to try again.

I think I was obsessed then with bringing home the bacon, the furniture, the second car, the home electronics, the exotic holidays. That's what I thought we both wanted, and we did set out loving each other; what else is there? I hadn't considered that merely gathering possessions doesn't make a marriage. Maybe there's a chance to forgive. Her, for the betrayal; me, for my insensitivity.

Goal

I have met my wife, and have spent the entire day with her, at a place we both like. We were both open, and kept our minds on the future, not the past.

We have reached a common understanding, after discussing what we both want from our relationship. We will soon make a decision to continue our marriage and to learn from our experience.

BUILDING A HOUSE

Background

I have a dream of designing and building my own house. My wife tolerates my sketching away on rainy Sundays, but avoids any discussion on what I'm doing. She doesn't want to acknowledge that I'm really serious. I have an obsession with this building project. But of course, it never gets off the ground, emotionally or literally. In my life, I haven't really achieved anything that I can "leave behind". I know it sounds a bit morbid and silly, but a house that I built would make people say, "Oh yes, Tommy built that house himself". Of course, I like the idea of having a house the way we want it. I'm sure my wife would suggest a floor plan. I've never built more than a small garden shed and a doll's house for Susan! So I've no experience, my wife would think I was nuts, and the upheaval would be horrible. So it's just another frustrated pipe-dream lacking credibility.

My dream is more than nonsense! Other people build their own homes. They admit it isn't easy, but where would the challenge be otherwise? I'm 48, so not incapable of sawing wood and hammering nails. I might need help with the foundations, bricklaying, plastering etc., but I could have a go at everything else, including plumbing and wiring.

Goal

I have spent the winter season reading all I could find on building a house. I prepared sketches, and discussed them with my wife and daughter. From there, I prepared drawings for planning permission, which I now have.

I have found and purchased a suitable building plot. All my spare time will now be dedicated to getting ready for a May start.

In each of the major categories of problematic goals, you will recognise the doors you would rather not enter. The more difficult your problems, the more sensitive you are going to be about facing them.

What if some snoopy person should see your "compromising" goal, even if you hide it in the cistern? Blackmail! That is the risk you must take, or commit the goal to memory after you burn the vital piece of paper!

Do exercise painful experiences on paper. Bring it all out. Bring out anger, disgust, shame, panic. Set up a dialogue with yourself to place the facts in front of you; then examine your feelings and possible paths forward. If you desire growth, suffer a little, then take heart and move on. Follow this with an Open Person's resolve to structure a goal to help you deal with it. Keeping these things tied up in little black bags is not helping you at all.

The Billy Graham Crusade was in town. Last time, in Calgary, I meant to go, but didn't. This time, in Vancouver, I thought I might go, but couldn't get motivated. My curiosity won: what drew people to see him?

It was frustrating in the downtown traffic, near the Terry Fox Stadium. Parking was another headache. I walked to Robson Street, to join the slow mass of people on their way to the stadium. Time was moving on. Dodging around people, I made some headway. But doing so was difficult and irritating.

A "Don't Walk" signal stopped the flow. One car sounded its horn to clear the busy junction. It added to my sense of rising tension. A badly-crippled man blocked my way to the kerb; his sticks were a nuisance. This would certainly slow everyone down. I drew level with him, one stick touching my left shin. I was hot and bothered. I bet Billy Graham didn't arrive like this!

I felt that strange presence you get when someone won't take their eyes off you. The fellow was staring at me. He was about twenty, handsome, athletic looking, but hopelessly immobile without sticks. He wore a leather bomber-jacket, an Eric Clapton tee-shirt, designer jeans and training shoes. The sticks seemed like a joke; they just didn't fit. All the while, he was looking at my tense face; relaxed, gentle, full of *concern*, smiling.

"Going....to....see Billy Graham?" I blurted, worried by his eyes.

"Yeah, sure thing. I'm going too. We're *all going* to see Billy Graham", as if he had the reply ready.

When the light changed, he called out to everyone "OK here we go!", and we all moved forward like children on an outing with teacher. I walked at his pace, one stick slapping my leg. We didn't speak, but I'd look at him now and then. Always the calm smile, penetrating eyes. His motion was difficult, excessive, an embarrassing spectacle. We parted company at the turnstiles. Handicapped people, Gate K; people like me, any gate but K.

Inside, I tried to take it all in. I thought it seemed better on TV, but here I was. The sound wasn't too good, but then the stadium was built for sports and rock concerts. I suppose it was just as I expected; Mr. Graham's talk was on target, as usual.

When people went forward at the end, I asked myself if I could really do that. It was good old American evangelism at its best, getting the better of the masses! I sat and observed, seeing the show out. Wheelchairs were pushed to the front and the prayer began. I closed my eyes. It was silent apart from the prayer, with a dull, repetitive noise, barely audible, in the background. Air conditioning perhaps. I opened my eyes, looked down, and saw the young man making his lonely way to the front. I watched him, calmly, smiling, feeling close to him, tears streaming down my face.

Spiritual matters are awkward to deal with in a popularly unspiritual social consensus. It really has become a personal affair. This unfortunately means it shouldn't be talked about in everyday circles, because the reception is often critical or hostile. When a person feels the need to express inner consciousness of a spiritual nature, there are very few outlets which welcome any sharing.

We are not just molecules and electricity; when a person considers the consequences of this grey possibility, the reaching out begins. If you want personal spiritual development, don't be ashamed to include goals directly related to your own growth. Please do not demand visions or miracles within this context! But do consider the goal setting process a suitable vehicle to focus these very personal wishes.

The other familiar but "difficult" personal goal area, is the field of sexuality. It is only appropriate that some attempt is made to address this one. It is not the intention of this book to solve the sex problems of the nation. An excellent reference for you, with no reservations and with great respect, are the excellent companion volumes of THE HITE REPORT by Shere Hite. This American lady blazed new trails by basing her books on extensive matter-of-fact questionnaires and well-ordered replies from respondents.

The Open Person and the issues of sexuality are indeed an interesting combination. Our social consensus has changed (so we are told), and being open is the key to coping with it all. At least, we can be open relative to our own consciousness. So choose your own way, not that of popular consensus, or the hype of promotional conditioning. There is so much distortion and half-truths out there to make you feel you have serious problems! Be aware of that, and be free to make constructive goals in this area, like any other.

SEXUAL MATURITY

Background

We have had a good marriage until recently. I have worked for the last two years, wanting an interest outside the home. Often we are both tired after a working day. My husband joined a rugby club six months ago, and since then, he has steadily believed he is becoming inadequate as a lover. More and more, he pushes the problem to the background. Whenever we do begin something, he becomes self-critical and everything stops. His point of reference is the macho-image of his rugby friends, I'm sure. He takes their shallow stud mentality too literally, and seems to be measuring his "performance" against their innuendo. He won't discuss it. He's ashamed and scared. I know that men have this performance thing, even an underlying fear of women, if they can't be in control. I can see it's a vicious circle.

Our relationship is deteriorating fast. We both avoid the problems by working more. We keep off the topic of sex, to maintain the status quo. It's a tidy but useless solution. I haven't stopped loving him. How can I reassure a man who feels he is no bloody good, if he can't perform as his friends say he should? We're in this together, and I want to help him through it.

Goal

I am patient and supportive with my husband, and always find ways of removing the pressures he places on himself. I am resourceful and sensitive in our lovemaking, replacing performance as an objective with fun and relaxation.

I am aware that as the pressures to perform are removed from our physical relationship, we will discover a closer, more open, and more mature marriage.

You can now appreciate what it means to be an Open Person. If you are to make real progress, you should merge those "awkward" goals into your list. Think about the *total picture you are trying to achieve.* Will you be a happy person in your material/personal goals, while there are burning issues pushed conveniently under the mat?

Very often, we cannot make progress because there are underlying, unpleasant things in our lives which prevent us from moving at all. How can we start a journey if our car is stuck in deep snow? We have to do some shovelling first! Wishful thinking and distortion of the truth cannot remedy the facts: you must work at the nasty ones too. If not, they'll be back to dampen your fireworks.

You had a nice, neat set of goals; now you have to tag on some uncomfortable ones. Simple, isn't it? Including a few more relevant goals should not disturb your calm. Your aim is to draw up a complete picture. There is nothing to be gained by including only the things that sparkle. You must make your list comprehensive, to get what you want.

There are perhaps more goal possibilities for you to examine. You might want to solve a substantial problem quickly, with no grand plan for the future. The same methods can be used. As you gain familiarity and confidence in the procedures, you can improvise as you wish.

How long is your goal list now? No firm restrictions have been placed on you, so you may have gone overboard. If the list has grown substantially because of these extra problem goals, it might be wise to do some weeding from the total. By carrying too many, you are apt to get bogged down. Your goals then receive less attention than they need. A total list of 20-25 goals is heavy going. Try to aim for 15-18, and put the others in your pending file.

Eleven   Success Can't Be Easy

Nothing great was ever achieved without enthusiasm.

Ralph Waldo Emerson

Success has become larger than life through popular misconception. Contemplating the nature of success results in many confusing reflections from our value system. The very things we are commonly urged to aim for can be surprisingly hollow. Success can be one of the shallowest pursuits on earth, if we have not understood its implicit meaning to our own precious lives. Success may be nothing more than a fancy in our individual and collective minds; an illusion in fact. Success may be owning a sea-going yacht, or curing a stammer. Success, if we would but admit it, is learning to discover and manage our own lives. You might take five steps forward in your personal growth goals, then be forced to take seven back. Learn to accept that five did indeed go forward. You might see a way to go ten tomorrow. That is success, just as much as owning a gleaming Porsche.

Keep every avenue open. Every day, set out determined to move forward just a little more, no matter what side of the bed you came out of. And rejoice in any success, large or small. Be thankful and mindful of personal growth, as well as material results. You will always find it easier to fall back to your old ways. Your inner doubts will urge you to retreat, to where life is safe and predictable. But when you do retreat, and you honestly feel that's no good either, you're making progress.

You must expect to fail too, sometimes. That is reasonable, especially when we rely on our rational, Conscious Mind too much. When it happens, don't go to pieces and curse the Universe. Learn to reflect on the situation. Strong people learn a great deal from mishaps and setbacks. Problems show us perspective and realism, in a world full of exacting standards and idealism. You might complain bitterly that you are not achieving results, saying things like : "Either the system I'm using is no good, or I'm a born failure". People are known to be impatient, very lazy, and spiteful if things don't go precisely their way. That's human. Recognise these things and take care when you want to punish yourself! Perhaps laziness is the single most persistent force of resistance to overcome. It is well known that personal growth requires work and attention. Laziness always lurks about, enticing us to go back to our safe, predictable, regressive ways. Apply the goal achievement methods honestly, and with a cooperative spirit. Then go with the flow, in faith.

Just getting through the average day successfully can be an exercise in pursuing success. What is a successful day? It is certainly not a day when you make everyone around you unhappy, because your day is such a stinker. The rest of the world may be having a terrific day, while you are convinced the world is out to defeat you. Attitudes make the day go round, for everyone in your day, and for you. Try having more successful days!

As a pilot, I love everything about flying. An aircraft is not a vehicle, it is a living thing we strap ourselves into. But some people don't agree with me.

I was enroute to San Antonio, Texas. The man beside me was an oil executive. When he got on, he complained that the aisle seat was taken. He argued furiously with the girl over FAA regulations, when he couldn't put his laptop computer up in the rack. The seat belt was twisted. He hated middle seats. He hated afternoon flights that were running late. And he particularly hated this airline's food.

I gave up smiling and nodding blanket agreement. In conversation, I told him I was a pilot. Somehow, we got onto the subject of water in aircraft fuel tanks. He latched on immediately. Those goddamned ground staff! Incompetent mechanics! I said it happened to me once, and I lost one engine for some minutes before a restart. He asked if the big ones ran any risk. I nodded. He stayed quiet for some time.

Suddenly, we entered violent turbulence and the power was cut to flight idle. The descent was rapid and engine power varied. Through the noise and shaking, the intercom said something about fuel. Down we went. The man was rigid, face white, hands gripping the armrests.

I knew we had a fuel stop in Denver, but busy executives only notice flight numbers. The Rockies cause a choppy layer there in spring. We got a quick straight-in approach, no waiting, hence the rapid descent.

I never did tell the man what I knew, but all the snacks and refreshments were received with a smile on the Denver-San Antonio leg. When we arrived, he turned sheepishly and said:
"I guess you thought I was kinda hard on that flight attendant, huh?"
I nodded in agreement.

Success is a frame of mind, and a feeling of achievement. What use to society the miserable millionaire? (Unless he becomes an admired philanthropist). Just as goals could be perceived as a naughty word, then success also comes under this unfortunate brush. Goals and success have not stood up well to the passage of time. Both words have been over-exploited through the seventies; they reflect the self-centred "me" generation. The Yuppy movement appears to carry on the self tradition in the eighties.

Words convey pictures, and should the pictures be misleading to your consciousness, you can find yourself chasing the wrong rainbows. If you can only see success as a large grey Rolls-Royce, a walled mansion, and glamourous people lolling about being cool, think again. Success is not a case of saying "Alright, I've done my goals and the subconscious stuff, now where's my mansion, fantastic friends, collection of the world's most expensive cars, Bell JetRanger....?" The important message here is to be discerning and independent in choosing your type of success. Don't blindly mimic the Hollywood folks or the Sloane Rangers, just because people tell you "that's success". Start the process from yourself outwards, not from the celebrities backwards.

Your ideas on success are going to be different from the man or woman across the road, also reading this book. They have their own views on everything anyway. (They probably think *you're* successful, and want to be just like you!). Or more to the point, they would never want you to know they're reading this type of book. Nor, for that matter, their ideas on success.

It would be nice for several people in this situation to meet; to discuss their ideas and their progress. Since it is all such a personal thing, that might be impractical. However, if people were truly Open Persons, who knows what might result? The different views of success would be a useful moderator of the group's attitudes and reason. Each person would end up with a more wholesome concept of success, without necessarily limiting goals and dreams. Such a forum would require trust and warmth between people. Our society has made us very competitive creatures: spilling your "secrets" to others might bleed the profits from your business idea, or disclosing personal fears might make you seem a right wimp in front of your local brush salesman. These are the risks, but then the person who risks nothing, does nothing....

Ask a teenager what success is. Ask a child. Ask your grandmother or an elderly friend. Ask some members of your peer group. Listen (say little) and learn. Where does your success picture stand now? You may compile a shopping list which probably includes: money, status, lifestyle, career, social standing, being liked, nice clothes, nice car, nice partner, beautiful kids, contentment, happiness, nice house, nice friends, good health, exciting interests, being interesting, peace of mind, purpose. Older people tend to focus on human, personal qualities, because their illusions on gathering possessions have largely faded. Young people go for the trappings and the sizzle. That's inevitable. I think wisdom plays its part, also the relative maturity and level of personal growth of the individual, regardless of age. Many people get stuck at teenage values and become very confused in their fifties.

You alone have defined success *for you*. Now you must live with it, *when it comes to you*. Be ready, because it's not very far away! Your consciousness has been alerted; the wheels are in motion. You have learned how to access the most powerful tool for helping you: *your own Subconscious Mind*. You will now see success slowly entering your life, as you have pictured it.

Doubts will creep into your mind all the time. There will be a curious tension between the "changing you" and the "old you". It may well cause you to feel physically drained at times (energy is involved in the interchange between progress and resistance). Success is a *difficult* thing to achieve, so fear of failure will be created in your consciousness as part of the process. (Life itself is difficult; that's why so many of us live fearfully, dreading what's round the next corner). Did I ever say that change leading to success would be a breeze? I *did* say you've got what it takes, even if you're convinced a wicked tide has left you marooned on a sandbank. Your "old you" ideas on success will try to judge things for you, then present a summary of "helpful" findings. "Success isn't for you, friend, it's too difficult/you're not the successful type/you'll go strange with that meditation stuff/you'll lose all your friends". Who are you listening to? Ah yes, it's the old Conscious Mind again! Reasoning away, putting all the data into neat piles and showing you it doesn't add up. Remember, the Subconscious Mind is your guardian and protector; the Conscious Mind is simply handy but a verbose bore. Choose to ignore the bore, and make a new friend of your subconscious. It alone can flush out the self-critical dialogue, and let you move towards your *deserved* success.

Notice yourself in all situations. *Never reduce yourself to a cog in someone else's wheel.* Let your subconscious watch over you; feel secure that all is well, that you'll always cope. Keep your big picture in mind, every day. Why don't you get one of those watches that will beep for you? Use it to prompt you every hour of the waking day; to remind you that indeed, you are there, the goals you have set are real, and you are thinking of them. Beep! What are you doing now? Beep! What is your plan? Beep! Can you say your goals? Beep! What progress have you made?

Change will demand new expectations of you, expectations now prompted by your subconscious. The rules *must change.* If you want a goal satisfied, then you must have change. Any difficulties will pale in significance compared to the success slowly coming into your life. Nothing worthwhile comes easy, *but you may be surprised just how easy the results do come.*

Imagine yourself with your complete list of goals fulfilled. There you are, feeling particularly glad with your perseverance and growth. But are you limiting yourself? Visualise ahead and consider. For example:

-Are you "saving" yourself in any way? Avoiding situations that would exercise some of your newly-acquired skills or qualities? If you wanted to overcome nervousness in public speaking and become a respected toastmaster, how many speeches do you make each week?

-Are you living up to your success by doing things consistently? Do you wear smarter, newer clothes, exploiting colours you never "allowed" yourself before? Why keep your best outfits in the wardrobe? You're alive, are you not? Then *be alive* and look successful in your smart clothes!

-Do you give freely, of things and of *time?* Are you clinging to all this success you created for yourself? People seldom want your money or your possessions. What people value more than anything, is your time. Spend time with those who need a gift of time.

-Are you in love with yourself, and *all* those around you? Why not? Do you smile at rain rather than scowl at it? Are you allowing bad habits to come back and mess things up?

-Has success closed your vision to certain things that are inconsistent with your picture of success? You are on a bus, a plane, the underground. Are you only glancing at the beautiful people? Find beauty in everyone: we are more than molecules and pretty faces, more than outward appearances.

-Do you like money, or are you in love with it? By all means, attract money in great abundance, but have you lost your awareness of what it is? Money is a gift, not a possession. Gifts pass from hand to hand. Use your money to spread your success, to give love and magic to another.

-Are you a little embarrassed of your success? Do you hide it from people, to avoid their questions? (How did she do it? How can he drive a BMW now?). Are you artificially pretending to be the same old person? No need to flaunt success in their faces, but recall the candle-under-the-bushel story. Limiting yourself is one side of the coin. The other side concerns exploitation of the powers you have discovered. It is best to respect your new knowledge rather than drive it for all it is worth.

-Have you extended your original boundaries of success, without developing further goals? You've made it, so everything must get bigger and grander! Really? You selected very specific things for your life; you focused on them, and used your subconscious to get them. Now you just add anything that looks good! Don't play games with success, or the processes you used to get there.

Before you investigated all this, you didn't know enough to get more from your life; you believed you had reached your point of incompetence. Now you see possibilities you couldn't even contemplate back then. Do you think you have all the answers now? Be careful, we never know all the answers.

Continue to help others. Little things are often enough. Hold the door open for someone; be courteous to a tourist; help someone in a wheelchair to negotiate a bad pavement. *Look for ways to help.* Don't sneak out of sight, telling yourself that some other daft mug will come along. Expect to be snubbed! Expect to be involved! Don't expect automatic gratitude! Expect to be singled out as a soft-soap who helps people needing help! *It can only add to your success. Think of it as a Universal Law. Give, and it all comes back multiplied.*

When you put your success on the level it deserves, you can begin to open up to the world about you, as a successful person. Nothing has changed, but your attitudes will allow you to share success. When you do things for others, and take a genuine interest in them, you leave an example in the world that makes it a better place. It's interesting how, years later, we recall a certain good turn that someone did for us. Very often, we gave them nothing in return, not even gratitude. These recollections are significant events in our consciousness. You will find that the more you open up to the world with your success, the more success you will enjoy. More pieces of the jigsaw that is life will be given to you.

Why be jealous of others, when you can improve yourself, and be successful in your own way? Don't copy or mimic the success of others. Their success is *theirs.* When you choose a pattern of success that suits you, it is even more wonderful. When you study the lives of great people, great musicians, singers or actors, they invariably had the dream of success from childhood. Whenever the dream actually began, *the dream was their passion.* They kept the dream in their subconscious, and they worked towards it. Nothing ever stood in their way, *especially not themselves.* The vision was alive, a deep, personal thing.

Success is a quality of life that has many aspects to it. It can mean much more than money and flashy cars. Become the person you really *want to be,* and enjoy a lovely car for what it is, no more. Nothing need deprive you of a possession you honestly desire in your life. But when flashy cars and images become the whole purpose of life, we must recognise the consequences of phoney substitutions: we become frustrated materialists and aimless hedonists.

Success to the unemployed is having a job. To others, it is having a better job. To others still, it might be getting out of a job and into a business of their own. Then some of them want to be filthy rich and lounge about, avoiding any effort at all!

Politicians are successful when they stay in office, more successful if they can be in the Cabinet. We vote for them because they promise us jobs, rising prosperity, better lives. The notion of promised goals, promised success, keeps us all going. The results are always safely in the future. It's a tidy system, very plausible, but can you wait for so many promises to happen? They do their best with the system as it is. Listen to them, yes, but act alone anyway!

The quality of your life is vitally important. What use a stable of the best racehorses and a houseful of priceless antiques, if you have lost your way in this confusing vale of tears? Mr. Jones may have a 12 metre satellite dish on his lawn, but is all the television in the cosmos going to make him happy? Success is hard to pin down, isn't it? Sometimes the most obvious questions are the most profound. The more you search for sensible answers, the more you go round the loop again.

So the choice is very much up to you. Success isn't easy. Don't assume you can eat all the cake, then announce that cakes are not the thing at all, but coconuts are. Defining what you want is difficult. Setting goals that *really mean something to you,* is difficult. Achieving those goals is difficult, *but not impossible.* No, nothing here is impossible.

The truth is, the choices and the process are moving targets. You must accept this and act accordingly. Stay open and aware. After some honest groundwork and silent meditation, *the appropriate things for you will fall into place.* Have faith that they will. You will enjoy your journey, scenery too. You'll have the right goals, and the right success.

Twelve   This is Not The End

We have studied together. You have been coached in understanding the mind. You are now in possession of a set of tools you may not have possessed before. Your basic desire to be honest with yourself has helped you to this point. So what are you going to do about it?

Until one is committed, there is hesitancy,
the chance to draw back,
always ineffectiveness.

Concerning all acts of initiative (and creation),
there is one elementary truth,
the ignorance of which kills countless
ideas and plans:

That the moment one definitely commits oneself, then
Providence moves too.

All sorts of things occur to help one
that would never otherwise have occurred.
A whole stream of events issues from the decision,
raising in one's favour all manner of
unforeseen incidents and meetings and material assistances,
which no man could have dreamed would come his way.

Whatever you can do or dream you can:
Begin it.
Boldness has genius, power and magic in it.
Begin it now.

Goethe

An embarrassing question: how old are you? Be honest! Have you ever talked to insurance men who deal in statistical life expectancy? This is a worthwhile exercise; we should refresh our minds every year, like a medical check-up. How many years do you think are available to you? It's such an odd topic that we pretend it isn't a question at all: it's just a joke. Strolling through a cemetery in a strange town has an even stronger effect; what did the departed make of their lives?

Life can only be the present and the future. The past is well and truly over. Two things are useless to a stricken pilot: the altitude above, and the runway behind. When you're in a crisis, or merely thinking about one, the past is real enough (like the runway); but can you make use of it? The present need not be some sort of penance for the past. So many people hug their albatrosses like teddy bears, dragging them everywhere, moaning away. "Oh, these albatrosses, I really must do something about them, they're so heavy. Perhaps next year".

The present should be very real to you. Here you are, reading away, trying to make up your mind as you go. How many silent meditations have you tried? Can you recite your goals? Only you can gauge your progress along this narrow path. *Now is the time* to apply all your senses and use what you *have* to greet the future. Of course, you are free to drop out at any point. But why not defy your laziness and see what's within your reach?

The future can be a magnificent unfolding of what you are struggling with at present. No matter what mess you are in, or how deep in a rut you believe you are, there's hope. You have the answers inside you, but you've been very good at wallpapering all those years, layer upon layer, never stripping off the past. What colour *are* your walls?

Tell yourself you are running your own life, like a small, very promising business. Happy is the man or woman who owns all the shares in his or her company! Stay open to all things, or you will miss opportunities that are waiting to be picked. You might notice a chance to supply a new service or product. A way to make your present family situation broader in scope, and thus more rewarding for you. The chance of making new friends beyond your usual circle, who might be able to help you or share experiences with you. Be a likeable person; be open to and tolerant of other people's peculiar ways, and amused by your own.

Stop being judgemental. Are you perfect? Put all that silly judging energy into learning your goals and focusing on them. You can ask questions and criticise till the cows come home; get to work on *your* answers. Visualise, dream, paint the future in bright colours.

You won't have to change your passport, or fear being cut out of Aunt Maud's will. You might be the same person in name and legal description, but you'll be more magnificent. Is that such a frightening prospect?

Should you need to, review and revise your goals, otherwise you might get out of focus. Go through the procedure: the background and goal statement. Life is change, so be open to changing your goals. Don't be obsessed by your goals, worrying over them like new albatrosses of the mind. Be content with small steps forward. Any progress today? Was that a little improvement in behaviour? Relax and take it all in. Don't try so hard that your Subconscious Mind decides to hibernate, leaving you to your twittering Conscious Mind. Enjoy the process; otherwise it's all a bore. Learn to turn the work into fun, not penance.

You might think you're so lost, you'll never find yourself. (Goals are for other people, not you). Alcoholism is a typical lostness. But then, most alcoholics do hear their inner voice whispering away. When an alcoholic *admits to a group* he is rock-bottom, the basic healing process begins. When you *declare* a problem, it's the first step in the solution. Honesty with yourself is a precursor of the coming cure. We are all potential failures, one way or another. Short-of-perfect can be construed as being a failure. It's a very negative word. We should all think about the ways in which we fail. Otherwise, the growth and success we desire will be frustrated, through assuming a vain sense of smugness. No need to become depressed by your failings: reflect on them and plan to improve.

My new secretary was a bit green at first. She prepared a letter file for me, with a call-up label:
LETTERS - FILE COPIES - F.R. FAILURE
My name was always a perennial spelling problem, but this one, I had honestly never seen before. Letters were filed and taken out, by several people. I thought she might be dyslexic. It was interesting to ask myself, every day I looked in the file, in which ways I was a failure. When I had exhausted my list weeks later, we changed the name. The office wags had their private joke, but I had begun the task of personal renovation.

A failure believes he will always have too much distance to make up, after the gun goes off. So he drifts off to the side and sits brooding in the changing rooms. This stems from a relative judgement, not by society, *but by himself.* If each day moves even the most hopeless failure forward an inch, then *tomorrow* will always be slightly better. Progress is progress, whatever way it happens. Bad things happen to all people. This does not imply you are a failure. Identifying all bad experiences as failures, or as evidence that you are doomed to suffer, is gross over-reaction. Learn to acknowledge successes, however small, and shake off gloomy thoughts about your failings. You are what you think in this regard, but plain old effort is required to realise progress in life.

Goals are set at all possible levels. To believe that goals only come in the Rolls-Royce/swimming pool variety, is ludicrous. You know what you want, so have your own fun getting it, whether it's breeding champion chinchillas or writing children's books. Many people concentrate *only* on personal goals. They actually make a goal not to pursue material goals! Too many possessions have ruined their lives and values! Pursuing the elusive gravy train of personal comfort and affluence, innocently labelled "lifestyle", will never satisfy the discerning person. Lifestyle safaris are sadly quite hollow and fragile in terms of real life-purpose and happiness. So choose wisely and individually. Then take your goals about with you everywhere. To the launderette, the board meeting, the Social Security office, church, football ground, ice rink, beach or bar; wherever you are.

Consider living your life as if you are leasing rather than owning it. When you rent a video-tape player, do you forget about it, or do you watch as many films as possible? The time with the machine and tapes is limited; see life the same way. If you don't make proper use of your life, you will eventually attract remorse to your state of mediocrity. Then panic. Fortunately, even panic has its good points. It will push you into doing something, like reading this type of book!

Understanding your mind is central to your progress. With respect, it's vital to get to grips with this mind business. If you have doubts, then consult books on psychology, psychotherapy or meditation, which specifically deal with the workings of the human mind. It is an unusual but intriguing interest. Please make the effort. It is worthwhile returning to the mind, as a topic for review. Some discussion may help your depth of comprehension.

Instead of someone saying "How do you do?", what if they asked "Who are you"? Your snappy reply would be your name, of course. So *your name is you!* Not content with that, they ask again. "Yes I know the two words you're called, but who *are* you?" This is where you've lost a little control. Straight away, your mind scuttles about trying to think of an intelligent answer for this peculiar person. After a while, your mind decides who you are. Protecting *itself,* it declares that *you* are pretty much *your mind* (ego and intellect), and proceeds to justify the hypothesis with suitably impressive words. Fortunately, you are a much greater person than your mind, and reality is not limited to the size or contents of your mind. The "mind" referred to is of course the Conscious Mind.

When you tell your Conscious Mind to shut up for a period, you can make friends with your Subconscious Mind. Once you have stilled the chatterbox, there is a new dimension awaiting you. Until you grasp this very simple truth, you will continue to limit your life and dreams. There's nothing scary about any of this: you won't be burnt at the stake or anything!

Your Subconscious Mind is very much part of your total reality. It communicates in little whispers of meaning, rather than in words. We commonly call it intuition, creativity, brainwaves or "something just clicked". Your Conscious Mind interprets the whispers, translating the details into words and images for you to work with. But don't always assume the Conscious Mind fully understood the message: it might be adding little bits like an office gossip.

Sharing goals with your Subconscious Mind, and listening for instructions some time later, is really a process of meaning, rather than words. Yes, you normally express yourself and generally think in terms of words. But don't recite your goals like a parrot orator, unable to continue if you drop your speech. As you get to "know" your goals, you will be able to transfer "meaning" to your subconscious, not a string of thought-words. Try to reach this level as quickly as possible. Your Subconscious Mind will be impressed if you can communicate in this way. It will respond more efficiently. Understanding higher levels of mind is your key to greatness.

I realised that French people thought in French, Chinese in Chinese, and old Sarcee Indians in their beautiful ancient language. While working in Norway, I studied children who could speak (and think) perfectly in two languages. Were their thoughts in Norwegian more clear to them than in English? They said no, but their parents believed thoughts in the native tongue were richer, more expressive.

Would it be possible to create and witness identical thoughts in a Greek waiter and an Icelandic fisherman? Probably not, I concluded. Then thoughts are quite useless as a universal experience of meaning! Thoughts are limited, and limiting, which tends to highlight the real inadequacy of the Conscious Mind. If we are our minds, then meaningful communication must be haphazard indeed. With others, and with ourselves.

I was sailing with friends off the San Juan Islands. The weather was lovely and warm, with a good sailing breeze. The sails were trimmed perfectly.

The wheel was light and easy. For some three or four minutes, we glided along in ideal conditions. Glenn Miller played from a cassette tape; the flag on the transom fluttered beautifully. We ate excellent sandwiches, and sipped refreshing, cool beer. The only sounds came from the boat's motion, and the music.

All at once, we stopped eating and sipping beer. In a collective moment, we stared at each other's faces, a quiet, common knowing in our eyes. A wonderful calm was upon us, an overwhelming sense of intense well-being. The boat, the weather, the music, our motion across the water, at a particular latitude and longitude on the same shared earth. All at the same instant of time; the same shared recognition of the curious moment by all aboard. Words or mere thoughts had no meaning for us whatsoever, at that instant. We were joint and several in our momentary understanding that mind was just a tiny part of the whole.

Oh yes, immediately afterwards, we tried to capture that common feeling in words and thought. It seemed the only sane thing to do, for we felt a sense of embarrassment at the loss of control. We had lost our minds together, for a few precious seconds!

As I write about this now, I feel the energy of that glorious few seconds has been lost to communication altogether. Words give a reasonable account of a boat in US waters some years ago, where the music of Glenn Miller and nice weather made five people feel good. The sum of the parts: Conscious Mind loves to belittle everything, beyond itself.

Now I acknowledge, somewhere inside myself (avoiding words), that I am a much larger person than molecules and mind. It is a reality, a potential within us all! We do have these little episodes of vision. I try to be open and friendly to them. I try to cultivate and use them to my benefit, today and every day.

So you are not your mind. Don't limit yourself, no matter what your intellect says! Once you realise you are more than molecules and Conscious Mind, you will begin to achieve more. Most people never get close to this realisation. Consider yourself wise, to seek truth as you are doing.

Sadly, most people couldn't care less about *who* they are, or what real potential they have. If people make no effort to investigate these things for themselves, then they have no option but to remain as they are. We are all responsible for our own lives, whatever political flag we wave to, whatever philosophy makes sense to us. Who can breathe for you, think for you? Gathering excuses and blaming the system is fun for those that seek handy answers to tedious questions. But does that relieve you of ultimate responsibility for each hour of your day? It's the horse and water phenomenon: if you won't open up and listen, the life you desire will pass you by.

To open up does not mean you will be weak and vulnerable. All you are doing is seeing yourself (and everything around you) differently. People will respect your inner strength, arising from your outward honesty and courage to be different. You will begin to respect yourself. Both the feedback from others and your own feelings will reinforce your resolve.

In our daily lives, so many things are taken for granted. We are courteous to strangers in a public place, but we forget to tell the old folks we love them, or partners, or children, or pets! Our bodies are treated just as badly. Only when they complain with pain or discharges do we even notice they exist. Perhaps the single thing we do occasionally celebrate is the mind. Even then, we only recognise the rather unsophisticated Conscious Mind. "Look, here's me! Yes, just look at my smart thoughts!" Give a thought to your loyal, discriminating, wholly-wise Subconscious Mind!

Don't keep your love in a safety deposit box at the bank: express it now (unfinished business after the death of someone special is avoidable). By being open about life, and the realities of its duration, you will learn to find simple ways of helping others. Do this gladly, even if they snub you or refuse to say thankyou. One day, *they will remember,* in a moment of crisis perhaps. Cause and effect is a mysterious process. No need to show off about what you do: just do it. It will help you in your goals, whatever they are. Don't look for direct links or spin-offs. Stay open to possibilities beyond "If I help him, I'll get to know his wife, who happens to be the treasurer....etc". Striving for success in isolation or as a mercenary will make you lonely; become a willing participant in the development of the bigger picture.

Never be content with mediocrity (unless that is your goal). If you are continuously unhappy, then there *must be a reason.* Find it, and create change which brings about improvement. Don't go about with dread in your mind. Oh yes, the proverbial bus might be waiting to knock you down, but don't whistle for it! If you want to start your business, try it and see. How will you ever know if it's feasible or not, if you don't give it a try? If you feel the urge to visit Nepal but your budget stops at Nottingham, focus on the possibilities of the project, not your despair. If you are nervous among people and withdraw at every opportunity, get to work on *what you would like to be....* confident, relaxed, well-liked. The dreamers are the ones to watch. We may not need to have much, but we can taste the exhilaration of life by the way we choose to live it. *Believe in yourself.* How many other people take a moment to unconditionally cast their votes for you? Why not vote for yourself?

People really can be in charge of their own lives; just like a business they own all the shares in. Rather than facing up to this exciting reality, we allow things to continue, just as they always did. In essence, *people wait for circumstances and other people to define their lives.* A family puts lifestyle before personal growth: the shallowness forces the children to despise their parents and forever shun success as meaningless. A job is lost: the world comes to an end. A relationship finishes: there are no alternatives. Brilliant ideas won't germinate: a dull life is all there is. This is the way many people live. It is easier to wait and see what falls from the sky, rather than act to change the future.

No situation is hopeless, and nobody has a situation that cannot be improved. Each one of us is a candidate for setting goals and implementing change. Individuals vaguely desire to do all this, but prefer to spectate the sport rather than play it. Why always watch the tables at Las Vegas or Monte Carlo? Get in with a small stake and see how it feels!

Just as each person can change the environment and circumstances they have control over, groups also have a strong synergy to do the same. Group progress is often stifled by the committee mentality. However, good things are happening, where groups of dedicated people are "getting there from here". That's better than boring everyone to tears by explaining why it can't be done. Witness the sincere dedication of Prince Charles. He has taken bold, practical and controversial steps to highlight the misery of Britain's inner cities. He has been an open critic of failed architecture which has left a stark legacy of depressing buildings. Depressing structures that kill the spirit of the people within. The Prince's Trust is another positive step forward. His visibility is that of an emerging Open Person we can listen to! There are many ways in which he stirs people to do something, rather than sit back for the next Government, or the next world, to sort it out.

Witness also the group synergy in a place like Easterhouse in Glasgow. Post-industrial depression is an ailment, not a plague, and the despair that was so clear in Easterhouse is lifting. How is that possible? Because people are *doing something* to change their perception and attitudes *within.* Unemployment of about forty percent sets the atmosphere, but the emerging spirit of the people will defy the statistics of gloom. Ordinary people there are deciding "This is it, here and now!" and taking the plunge to build self-confidence and community respect again. The Easterhouse Festival encouraged people to confront despair with hope. Creative events such as photography, video and music were promoted. This enabled a return of the feeling that life is still worth living. Battles with officialdom have been largely circumvented by forging boldly ahead, against all the odds. It is a living project, an example of people consciously deciding to take a chance. There is nothing to lose but the boredom from watching stagnation. Groups or individuals, the rules are the same.

You will never achieve the things you want for your life by clinging to the past. You may have believed those things of the past gave you purpose, direction, a good life, security, balance, and personal unassailable integrity. Without flushing everything away, you can safely remove your instinctive will to "make do". Are you unhappy, unfulfilled, uneasy with life as it is? Why must you go on like that? Have you decided that life is a punishment of some sort? Unpleasant things and setbacks *hit us all,* but don't waste the rest of your life analysing them. Learn from them; then move on.

Focus on the goals you have given such personal care to. Begin to live them *now,* as if they have arrived! You have learned how to break the fog about you, so don't draw it back again! Change at a pace you can handle, and give some thought to those close to you. They might not be spinning at your speed. Stick with your inner resolve to *complete what you have started.* Be a finisher, not a butterfly.

Stop comparing yourself with others, above or below your station. Focus on yourself, but selflessly. Be honest with yourself and other people. Live in the moment and live it to the edges. Whatever you do is important, whether it's thrilling or mundane. Learn to laugh at yourself; you really can be funny! Be your own person, strong and resolute; refuse to be compromised or debased through some silly diversion, or criticism. If you have good ideas about something, collect them and use them. Develop the facility of exchanging ideas with your Subconscious Mind. Begin to trust your *inner support system.* Stay open, whether it yields exciting work possibilities, healthier relationships, or clearer understanding of others and the world we live in.

Define the life you want, and achieve it. What else are you here for? Never be too proud or scared to try. Consciously vote to enjoy life, despite the negative press. See the possibilities and move towards them. You alone are in command of your choices, your destiny; you are free, always. There must be more than you allowed yourself in the past. Now is the time to find it.